The Non-Competitive
Activity Book

The Non-Competitive

Activity Book

Robin Dynes

Published by
Speechmark Publishing Ltd,
St Mark's House, Shepherdess Walk, London N1 7BQ, United Kingdom

© Robin Dynes, 2000
Reprinted 2001, 2003, 2004, 2005, 2006, 2009, 2014

002-4125/Printed in the United Kingdom by Hobbs the Printers

British Library Cataloguing in Publication Data

Dynes, Robin
  The non-competitive activity book
  1. Games – Therapeutic use
  I. Title
  793

ISBN-13: 978 0 86388 372 9

Contents

Introduction

The non-competitive games and activities in this book can be used across all age groups and disciplines. They will be particularly useful with learning disabilities, mental health, physical disabilities, regressed psychiatric patients, elderly and geriatric patients.

Why non-competitive games and activities?

Non–competitive games and activities:
* Avoid reinforcing a negative self-image;
* Ensure that there is no disappointment at not 'winning';
* Enable people to participate without fear of failure or thinking of themselves as a failure: there is no need to feel threatened or anxious, they know their sense of self-worth will not be damaged;
* Make it easier to become involved because there is no threat of failure or rejection;
* Ensure enjoyable experiences because there is no threat of failure or rejection;
* Generate a greater feeling of acceptance, co-operation and sharing, which helps to build trust, a sense of safety, comfort and self-esteem;
* Enable people to empathise better with each other, be concerned about each other's feelings and get along better together;
* Ensure that everyone feels safe when they make a contribution;
* Promote a spirit of support and sharing.

Competitive games and activities:
* Can be rigid, judgmental and very goal orientated;
* Give only the winners approval, acclaim and prizes;
* Can encourage winners to take delight in the failure of others and to tease or taunt them;
* Promote the idea that losers are less well thought of, which often leads them to see themselves as failures or inadequate. They become demotivated, frequently give up and may see themselves as being disapproved of or rejected;
* Can lead to the importance of winning taking priority rather than enjoyment of the activity;
* Can lead to a lack of sensitivity to other people's feelings;
* Can lead to people learning to avoid competition and withdraw rather than reinforce a negative concept of themselves;

* Have the potential to be destructive rather than a positive reinforcing experience for those who are not 'winners';
* Are less likely to succeed in helping someone who is depressed or withdrawn to feel safe, build trust and confidence and become involved.

The above factors make non-competitive games acceptable and useful within all settings – particularly so when individuals are depressed or withdrawn. Activities feel safe and trust is built. Individuals become involved in the process of reacting, feeling and experiencing. Curiosity is aroused, thought and creativity are ignited which in turn encourages involvement in working out solutions to problems.

In the safe environment people feel free to offer suggestions and to make decisions and choices. Motivation is greatly enhanced. People feel more important and have a greater sense of personal control. Carers are also enabled to listen to individuals' feelings and perspectives and to respond to these.

Using the book

This book contains one hundred games and activities, with many more variations. These are divided into sections.

Section 1: **Starters and Pairing Up Games**
Section 2: **Movement**
Section 3: **Perception**
Section 4: **Cognitive Stimulation**
Section 5: **Endings**

These sections, used in sequence, provide a format for complete sessions. Activities, one from each section, go together to make a complete session. The session starts with an introduction or warm up exercise to help group members relax and get to know each other and to enable the group to begin a cohesive process. This is followed by activities in the areas of movement, perception and cognitive stimulation. Endings are provided to wind down the group and bring it to a close. Alternatively, activities can be chosen as required from any section, in any order or combination, to meet identified needs of individuals.

The materials needed for each game are given, together with any preparation required, the procedure and variations on the theme. Comments are provided as useful hints about the use of each game. Most of the activities can be made easier or more difficult as required and some suggestions are offered to facilitate this. Some of the exercises could equally be used in different sections.

The activities are not intended to be exhaustive: add your own ideas or 'mix and match' as you see fit. The games presented are meant to stimulate ideas – many other books are available from Speechmark, among others, from which you will be able to choose more activities, fitting them into the structure provided here. This enables your group to change to meet client need, to keep it interesting (for both you and the group) and to use your own creativity. However, you will need to take care to remove any competitive elements when choosing activities from other sources.

Some issues to bear in mind

PLANNING THE GROUP

Although the format of the group is suggested you will still need to do some planning. Give some thought to the activities you choose and adapt them to meet the needs of your group. You should take the following into account:

* Physical and mental abilities;
* The individual needs of each person;
* Group cohesion;
* The activity level within the exercise (whether a less active exercise should follow an active one);
* The ability of group members to concentrate;
* The size of the group;
* Group members' expectations;
* How one session builds on another;
* Location and time of day the group meets. This should ensure that the group is not interrupted and is at a time of day when everyone will feel rested and reasonably fresh;
* How long the session will last;
* Frequency of the sessions – it may be more effective to meet often, for example, daily rather than weekly, for short periods.

As the session progresses, do not be afraid to adjust your plan: the needs and mood of the group may become more apparent as the exercises proceed. Modify or change your plan to suit. When explaining an activity, be clear about the purpose of doing it. Just how detailed or simple your explanation is will be dictated by the degree to which group members are withdrawn and by their abilities to concentrate. Ask if instructions have been understood and restate points as necessary.

Seating

Sitting in a circle with everyone facing inwards is the best way to ensure that everyone can see each other, make eye contact and be aware of what is going on. However, this can be varied. If abilities allow, you may sometimes be able to form a circle with everyone standing, or to seat them around a large table.

There is a tendency for people always to sit in the same place. You could ask participants to make eye contact with someone and change places. This way they will perhaps get to know someone new while doing the next exercise. This all adds a little variety to the process. Do be aware, though, that routine establishes familiarity and a sense of security. Enough variety needs to be present to stimulate and create interest but not to confuse or threaten.

Using the format

STARTERS AND PAIRING UP GAMES

Choosing a starting exercise will ensure that the group begins with an exercise which provides an 'alerting for pleasure' experience to help people relax, get to know each other and begin a cohesion process. With regressed or unresponsive people it is a good idea for the group leader to start by speaking to individuals by name, making a small comment and touching them by either shaking or holding their hand. As individuals wait to be approached their anticipation will be aroused. It gives pleasure to have your name spoken and to make physical contact. Also people are recognised as individuals.

Another simple beginning is to have each person turn to their neighbour on their left and right, shake hands and greet them with 'good morning, pleased to see you' or some such appropriate pleasant greeting.

Doing either of the above or the exercises provided to start the group can help you to gauge the mood of the group and decide if you need to make changes to activities chosen for the session. It can establish routines with which people become familiar for each session and help people who do not know each other to become acquainted and feel more comfortable.

Some of the exercises will also be helpful to use for pairing people up when this is desirable.

Movement

The aim of this section is to help enhance a positive self-image, assist non-verbal communication and facilitate emotional response. The exercises will also help maintain or increase physical tone, posture and well being. Depending on abilities, these activities may need to start at a slow pace and do not necessarily have to be done in a vigorous manner. They should be presented in a non-critical manner. Make clear that each person should only do as much as they are able and can stop when they wish after making a reasonable attempt. Do make sure that, in the choice of activity and its adaptation, account is taken of participants' overall physical condition, specific disablements and mental functioning. It may be essential to start very gently and make slow progress. The activity should be a natural follow-on from the chosen opening.

Perception

These activities aid sensory stimulation, promote awareness of the world and how individuals perceive it and themselves in relation to it. They also prompt memory and emotional associations.

If the previous exercise has been very active, choose a slower activity from this section. Encourage any discussion that stimulates people to remember things from the past. Bear in mind when doing the activity that asking people to volunteer or hand objects to another chosen person encourages them to make decisions and move around.

Cognitive stimulation

Most activities lead to producing organised thought. The emphasis here is on creative activity, opportunity for problem solving and decision making.

Endings

Endings should bring events to their natural conclusion and reinforce what has been good about the group. Calmness and a feeling of satisfaction should exist along with the opportunity to give a natural response to a pleasant time spent together. Sensitivity and good timing are required. Skill in achieving this can only be gained through experience.

Using the above format for each session will ensure that you pay attention to the functioning of the whole person. However, there may be times when you choose to use one exercise on its own or to leave out a section to allow more time to concentrate on particular needs. This may be influenced by the length of time that the group gets together and the pace at which the group is able to work.

Avoiding problems

* Not everyone may feel able to participate or respond. The person can still be included in the circle or encouraged to sit just outside it, wherever they feel comfortable. They can then be included in the activity as they are able to respond. Usually, they will gradually do so. Even if they do not participate they will still be stimulated by what is going on.

* Be aware that many things can affect the group. These may include bad nights, changes in people's lives, new staff, new admissions, depression, anxiety, feeling threatened, the time of day the group is run and so on.
* The exercises are designed to counteract isolation, loneliness and deprivation when people are mainly related to on a duty basis. Do not drop activities because they are not at first successful – especially when working with people who are withdrawn. Simplify the procedure if necessary and try it again so that you can understand why it is not working. Alternatively, present it in a different way, or ask the group why they do not like it. They will very likely tell you. The mood may not be right on a particular day or more time or repetition may be needed for it to be effective. Hostile remarks or abandonment by participants may mean the activity has been presented in a way that is too threatening. Many of the exercises can be done with individuals on their own, and this helps them build confidence and work towards participating in the group. It may be that, rather than abandoning the exercise, you have identified an area of need, on which more work needs to be done.
* Regressed individuals need much more than instructions to make activities successful. Use touch, nearness, a calm voice and eye contact to facilitate response. Move around the group members, encouraging them to get involved with each other.
* Do not force yourself on people. Ask why they feel the way they do or what they dislike about what you are doing. Offer the activity again in a way that is acceptable to them. This gives opportunity for group leaders to learn from participants and helps promote a bond of trust.
* Repeat people's names often and address them in a personal way which identifies them as individuals.
* Participate fully in all parts of the exercise. Volunteer to take a turn.
* Help individuals to participate and volunteer ideas if someone is passive.
* Be ready to move on if group members are becoming bored.
* If it is difficult for someone to share personal experience with the group help them by making innocent, appropriate, self disclosure.
* Share the group leadership with participants as much as possible.

Ensuring success

The fact that all the activities are non-competitive removes threat and encourages co-operation. The format ensures that stimulation is provided for all the major areas of functioning. The combination of non-competitive games and the suggested ways to use them for sessions provides maximum opportunity for success. It will promote the well being of group members and maintain and improve functioning in an atmosphere of fun and enjoyment.

SECTION 1

Starters and Pairing Up Games

A selection of non-competitive opening and pairing up games. These are activities which can act as ice-breakers, arouse interest and prepare participants for what is to follow.

Guess Who?

Materials

Pens, paper and a bag.

Preparation

None.

Procedure

Give each group member a pen and some paper. Ask them to write down three things about themselves. This might be:

1 Where they were born.
2 A hobby or game they enjoy.
3 A job they have done.

Alternatively, give group members freedom to choose three things about themselves they do not mind sharing. When everyone has finished writing, collect all the pieces of paper and place them in a bag. Now have someone draw out one of the pieces of paper and read out what it says. The group members then try to guess who wrote the three things. Allow a limited number of guesses before the right person owns up. When they do, encourage them to expand on what has been written and get the other group members to ask questions. When this has been exhausted have someone else draw out another piece of paper and follow the same procedure. Continue in this manner until all have been identified. Do warn people that if they pick their own piece of paper, they should read it out without acknowledging it is theirs until other group members have had a chance to guess who has written it.

Variations

1 Ask group members to write down three likes and three dislikes and then proceed as above.
2 To simplify, dispense with the writing and simply ask each person to state their name and three things about themselves.

Comment

You can, of course, ask each person to write down more or fewer details about themselves. This is a good exercise to encourage people to share information about themselves as they get to know each other – often, shared interests or experiences are revealed.

Getting to Know You

Materials

Cards or sheets of paper and pens.

Preparation

Prepare a list of six questions, for example:

1. What is the name by which you like to be known?
2. What is your favourite TV programme?
3. What irritates you most?
4. What makes you smile?
5. Who do you most admire?
6. What is your favourite meal?

Procedure

Give each person a card and a pen. Ask them to write the numbers one to six in sequence down the left hand side of the card. Now ask the prepared questions and have everyone write down their answers. When these are completed, request that each person passes their card to the person on their left. Group members, in turn, now introduce the person on their right to the whole group reading the information from the card. Encourage people to explain further about what is being read out and other group members to ask questions.

Variation

Instead of using cards start by having a round with everyone stating their name. Then have another round with everyone, in turn, answering the second question. Next ask the third question. Continue in this manner until all the questions have been asked. Use each person's name every time you ask them a question. Encourage each person to expand on their answer to each question.

Comment

You can, of course, use fewer than six questions. The questions can be changed to suit any group or be used several times with the same group. This is a good ice-breaking activity which encourages the sharing of information. Carefully thought out questions to suit the group can reveal the most amazing things.

Half-a-Picture

Materials

Some magazines and scissors.

Preparation

Cut out pictures from magazines or a similar source. Cut each picture in two, jigsaw fashion. If you have 10 players in the group, you will need five pictures – half a picture for each person.

Procedure

Make sure the half pictures are well jumbled and give them out at random, one piece of picture to each person in the group. Ask participants to find the person with the other half of their piece of picture and, when they find the other person, ask them to introduce themselves, have a chat, and find out the other participant's name and at least two things about them. Once this has been completed, assemble everyone again in a group with the pairs together. Now have players show their pictures, one pair at a time, and then introduce their new friend to other members of the group.

Variations

1   Cut the pictures into three or four pieces. This will enable small groups to be formed who can chat to each other. When ready the members of the smaller groups can take it in turns to show their picture and introduce each other to the main group.

2   If group members are familiar with each other, choose interesting or comic pictures, which can then be discussed by the pairs when together. Their thoughts on it can be shared with the whole group later.

Comment

A pleasant introduction or warm-up activity for groups, this always goes down well. It can also be used for pairing people up in preparation for another activity.

Representative Feelings

Materials

None.

Preparation

None.

Procedure

Everyone sits in a circle. Ask group members to think of an animal which best represents how they feel at present. After a moment for thought, have people, one at a time, state the animal which represents how they feel. Encourage each person as they make their statement to expand on it. What is it about the animal which expresses their feeling? Most will be pleased to expand on their own answer, but do not force this if anyone is reluctant to do so, some may wish to merely state the animal.

Variations

1   Ask people to name an object which represents how they feel.
2   Ask people to name a flower which represents how they feel.
3   Ask people to name a piece of furniture which represents how they feel.
4   Ask people to name a bird which represents how they feel.

I am sure you can think of many other theme subjects which could represent feelings.

Comment

This is a simple method of enabling people who may be reticent about stating their feelings, or who may have difficulty putting their feelings into words, to have the means to do so.

Name Game

Materials

None.

Preparation

None.

Procedure

Have the group members sit in a circle. Invite each person, in turn, to state their name. When this has been completed start a second round. This time members put a descriptive adjective before their name which represents how they see themselves, such as: sensitive Joy, jolly Peter, quiet Susan, fun-loving Jack, and so on.

Variations

1   When you do the first round of names, have the first person state their name. The second person then states the first person's name and their own. This continues round the circle until the last person says everyone's name. The process can then be repeated, adding the qualifying adjectives.
2   Have individuals use a descriptive word beginning with the first letter of their name. For example: pretty Paula, jolly Jack, laughing Laura, sharp Sheila and so on.
3   Have the group members state their name and one word which best represents them at present. For example: sad Bill, fed-up Jill, bored Jane, joyful Chris, hopeful Paul, and so on.

Comment

This game is easily adapted to suit group abilities. It is also very useful in helping group members remember each other's names, as well as enabling them to state how they feel. It is fun, too, and is a good introduction exercise to arouse people's interests in preparation for another activity.

Sayings

Materials

Blackboard and chalk or a flipchart and magic markers.

Preparation

None.

Procedure

Ask the group members to call out some of the things that their parents, grandparents or teachers used to say to them when they were young.
Examples are:

* Don't talk with your mouth full.
* Waste not, want not.
* Stand up straight.
* Take your time.
* Give yourself a chance.
* Stop biting your nails.
* Smarten yourself up.
* Forgive and forget.
* Use your head!
* Watch your tongue!

Encourage individuals to talk about the person who made the comment and why. Did the comment influence them in any way? When you have a good selection of the sayings on the board, invite everyone to go round greeting other members of the group by supplying their own name and using one of the sayings. For example: 'I'm Joe, pull your socks up my lad.' Individuals may use the same or different sayings for each person greeted. If group members are well acquainted with each other, have them say the name of the person they are greeting and the saying. For example: 'Hello, Jane, take your time.' End the exercise by having a short discussion on how it felt to be greeted with the saying.

P

Variations

1   Instead of sayings use well known proverbs. Examples: 'It is all in a day's work', 'Every dog has his day', 'Practice makes perfect'.

2   Instead of sayings use catch-phrases. Examples: 'Come up and see me sometime', 'Who loves ya, baby?', 'Where were you when the lights went out?'

3   Instead of sayings use song titles. Examples: 'The Yellow Rose Of Texas', 'Stand By Your Man', 'Do Ya Think I'm Sexy', 'These Boots Are Made For Walkin''.

Comment

This is another enjoyable way to help people learn each other's names and to break down barriers. Even when names are not remembered, the process of introduction changes the psychological configuration of the group: people become more relaxed in approaching and talking to each other.

Eye Contact

Materials

Some soft background music, tape or CD, and player.

Preparation

None.

Procedure

Play some soft music in the background. Ensure that everyone is sitting in a circle. Ask everyone to glance around the group in an attempt to make eye contact with another person. This can be the person opposite or to either side. Once eye contact has been made, the two people exchange places while still keeping eye contact. For a first round, have people do this in silence. For a second round, have the two people making eye contact exchange a greeting and state their name as they pass in the centre. Greetings can be kept simple, such as : 'Hello, my name is Barbara' or 'Pleased to meet you, my name is Bill'.

Variations

1   If people are familiar with each other have them name the other person as well as saying a greeting. This might be: 'You're looking well, Doris' or 'Isn't it a lovely day, John?'
2   Use the game to divide members into pairs. When eye contact is made, people pair up, exchange names and then introduce their partners to the whole group ·or proceed to another activity requiring the group to be subdivided into twos.

Comment

This is a good activity to help 'reconnect' people who avoid looking at each other. Also people like to be addressed by name. It is difficult to make eye contact, pass a greeting and not smile. If group members are not mobile, they can make eye contact, wave and make a greeting.

Complete the Statement

Materials

None.

Preparation

None.

Procedure

Ensure that everyone is sitting comfortably in a circle. Invite someone to complete the statement:

'My name is _____ The best thing that happened to me this week was
_____ ,'

When the statement has been made encourage the person to expand on what has been said. When this has been exhausted, invite another person to complete the sentence. Continue in this manner until everyone has had an opportunity to make a statement and expand on it.

Variations

Other beginnings for statements could be:

1   The worst thing that happened to me this week was
_____

2   If I were an animal I'd be
_____

3   If I were a piece of fruit I'd be
_____

4   If I had last week to live over again I would
_____

5   What I'm looking forward to today is
_____

6   If I were a piece of furniture I'd be
_____

7   The best thing that ever happened to me was
_____

Opposites

Materials

Slips of paper and a bag.

Preparation

Cut up slips of paper. Write a word on one piece of paper and its opposite on another.

Examples:

large	small	loss	gain
hot	cold	generous	mean
thick	thin	win	lose
wide	narrow	specific	general
dark	light	cheerful	gloomy
quiet	noisy	end	beginning
optimist	pessimist	up	down
scarce	abundant	below	above
oppose	co-operate	concrete	abstract
continue	cease	reject	accept
loose	tight	modern	old-fashioned

P

near	far		young	old

genuine	artificial		happy	sad

weak	strong		friend	enemy

flat	steep		dull	shiny

dry	wet		smooth	rough

Prepare slips of paper equal to the number of group members.

Procedure

Give each group member a slip of paper or have them take one from a bag. Each person then seeks out the person who has the opposite word to the one they have selected. When they have found their partners, have them chat to each other for a few minutes to find out a couple of details about each other. Now have the group come back together and each pair introduce their partner to the whole group.

Variations

Instead of opposites use:

1 famous couples,
2 a word and its meaning,
3 question and answer.

Comment

This game can also be used as a pairing up activity in preparation for another exercise. It provides an amusing way for people to get to know each other.

Novelty Basket

Materials

A basket and a number of old or novelty items such as an old photograph of the area, a monocle, a hat, a postcard, a whistle, a mousetrap and so on. Ensure variety in size and weight and that the objects are age appropriate.

Preparation

Place all the items in the basket.

Procedure

Invite one person in the group to pick out an object. Give them time to examine what they have chosen and then ask them to comment on it to the rest of the group. Why did they choose it? Does it remind them of something? Do they like the item? Encourage them to examine the article and pass it round to other members of the group to share thoughts about it. When one item has been exhausted invite another group member to choose another item and go through the same procedure. Continue in this manner until everyone has had a turn.

Variation

Instead of having one group member choose an item, pass the basket round and have everyone choose one. Now give each person, in turn, an opportunity to share and discuss their item with the whole group.

Comment

This activity provides good proprioceptive and tactile input as the items are examined. It helps to arouse a sense of pleasure and can be particularly useful with people who have regression symptoms.

Auto-biography

Materials

A watch or stopwatch.

Preparation

None.

Procedure

Have the group sit in a circle. Request each person, in turn, to state their name and give a brief autobiography. They may start: 'My name is Mary Curtis. I was born in Belfast. I left school at 15 and went to work in the local linen factory as a machinist.' The person continues in this fashion for a set time – one or two minutes. Warn participants that they will be stopped when their time is up. Indicate that time is running out a few seconds before the limit so that individuals can round off what they are saying.

Variations

1   Each person shares a success story. This may be passing an examination, successfully purchasing a sought after item, choosing the right colours for a room, meeting the right person at the right time, being in the right place at the right time or preparing a special meal.
2   Each person talks about their strongest personal asset and how this has affected their life. This may be pride in a job well done, a caring nature, a sense of humour or determination.

Comment

If your group is really large you can break it up into smaller groups of five or six people with one person being an appointed timekeeper. This prevents the activity going on too long.

Dolls

Materials

Make or buy 2, two to-three feet (60–90 cm) tall cloth constructed dolls – one male, one female. Each doll should be appropriately dressed. Give the dolls accessories such as a handbag and briefcase.

Preparation

None.

Procedure

Introduce the dolls to the group and explore how they are made. Pass them round one at a time so everyone can have a good look, feel the material and so on. The process of doing this will likely spark off conversation and memories. Next ask each person if they remember a favourite person they can imagine one or both of the dolls to be. Have people expand on this and then ask: 'Is there anything you would like to say to him or her?' Follow this with: 'What do you think they would answer?' You can also ask: 'What do you think they would have in their handbag /briefcase?'

Variation

Use the two dolls together – male and female. Ask the group to give them names and create a relationship between them. Have the group use their creative imagination to build a life story for the dolls. Different groups and, indeed, the same group on different days, will create different stories, especially if you make small changes to the dolls' appearance. This variation can be used on its own or as a follow on from the initial exercise.

Comment

This is a very useful exercise to use with regressed clients. The response is well worth the time, effort and cost of the dolls. A few people may initially reject the dolls, but usually they will gradually accept them. Do not thrust the dolls on anyone who is at first reluctant. Give time for them to observe others handling and talking about them and most will eventually join in.

Feeling Mime

Materials

Blackboard and chalk or a flipchart and magic markers.

Preparation

Make a list of feeling words such as exhausted, sad, joyful, sleepy, irritable, depressed, content, hungry, angry and so on. Now work out how you are going to act out each word in an exaggerated manner.

Procedure

Place yourself where you can be seen by everyone and act out one of the feelings listed. The group members have to guess what the feeling is. This can be followed by asking if anyone feels like that at present. Give an opportunity for anyone to expand on this if they wish, before moving on to the next feeling.

Variation

Ask group members to act out how they are feeling in an exaggerated manner. For example, if someone feels sleepy they could close their eyes and pretend to snore. If happy they could give a big smile.

Comment

This activity is good fun and produces unexpected responses and results.

Seasonal Feelings

Materials

Blackboard and chalk or flipchart and magic marker.

Preparation

None.

Procedure

Seat everyone so that they can see the flipchart and write a season or point of the year on the chart. This may be autumn, winter, summer, spring, Christmas, Easter, the longest day of the year and so on. Ask group members to call out any feelings they associate with the time of year chosen and write them on the chart. Give plenty of opportunity for each person's feeling and association to be explored. Ensure that everyone has an opportunity to contribute at least one feeling. When this is completed, write another season on a clean flipchart sheet and go through the same procedure again. Continue in this manner as appropriate, and as time allows.

Variation

Write a season on the flipchart and have each person state one like and one dislike about it. Repeat for each season as appropriate.

Comment

Discussion can be directed to expand into personal experience of events from group members' lives associated with particular seasons of the year or general discussion about celebrations or memorable events attached to seasons, such as weddings, spring fashions, very hot summers and so on.

P

Feelings Cards

Materials

Card, magic markers.

Preparation

Cut up a large number of cards. Using the magic marker, write a different feeling on each one. Examples:

angry	happy	grumpy
pretty	sad	relaxed
anxious	confident	embarrassed
drowsy	wide awake	sleepy
restless	irritable	comfortable
uncomfortable	worried	tired
amused	indifferent	displeased
relieved	hopeful	lazy
silly	weak	nervous
ignored	valued	argumentative
tense	afraid	respected
lonely	helpless	controlled

Procedure

It is usually best to have everyone sit in a circle. Hold up each card in turn and state what the feeling is on the card. As you call out each feeling, ask group members to take the card if it reflects how they are feeling at that moment. Give each person their chosen card, so that they can hold it to be seen by everyone. Give an opportunity for each person to share and expand on why they are feeling a particular way. For some it may be enough just to acknowledge the feeling. It is useful to have some extra blank cards ready, as more than one person may be feeling the same way or the feeling words chosen may not 'hit the spot' exactly for everyone. These can then be written on as required.

Variations

1 Give each person a blank card and a magic marker. Have them write a word which expresses what they are feeling. When this has been completed, have each person, in turn, hold up their card and state their feeling. Again, encourage them to expand on their feeling, as appropriate.

2 Brainstorm feeling words on a flipchart and then have each group member select a word which expresses how they are feeling at present.

Comment

This is an activity which adapts well to people who do not give much response or have regressed. Some people, especially if they give little response, are usually only asked if they are OK or if they are sick.

Something in Common

Materials

None.

Preparation

None.

Procedure

Ask group members to approach other individuals in the group and find someone who likes the same colours as they do. Encourage them to share what they like and dislike about various colours and ask each other questions. When each person has had time to find someone with similar taste and have a brief discussion, bring everyone back together again and invite members to introduce their partner to the whole group recounting what they have found out about them.

Variations

1   Ask group members to find someone else:

*   with the same colour eyes,
*   with the same colour shoes,
*   who likes or dislikes the same sort of food,
*   who likes the same TV programmes,
*   who likes the same sport,
*   who likes the same season of the year,
*   who likes the same sort of flowers,
*   who likes the same sort of music.

2   When players have found someone with the same colour eyes, allow time for them to chat for a moment. Now ask everyone to find someone else with the same colour eyes. When this has been achieved, ask them to find someone with the same colour shoes. Continue in this manner as long as is appropriate.

Comment

Many other non-threatening personal preferences can be used in this manner to enable people to pair up, exchange interesting facts about each other and help get to know each other. Of course, you do not need to end the activity by having group members introduce each other to the group if they already know each other, or if you just want to pair people up for another activity.

Musical Names

Materials

A bean bag or soft ball, music tapes, CD or records and something to play them on.

Preparation

Have the music ready to play.

Procedure

Have everyone sit in a circle. Start the music playing and the players passing the bean bag from one person to another. At an appropriate time stop the music. The person now holding the bean bag states their name and something they like. For example: 'My name is Alice and I like going shopping.' The music is started again and the bean bag is passed around again until the music is stopped once more. This procedure is followed until everyone has had an opportunity to state their name and something they like at least once.

Variations

1　Do one round of 'My name is _____ and I dislike _____'
2　Start the group with a round of 'My name is _____ and I like _____', then switch to using 'dislike' for a round.
3　Use other specific topics. For example:

  ✱　TV programmes,
  ✱　favourite songs,
  ✱　food,
  ✱　famous people,
  ✱　sports, and so on.

Comment

This game can be simplified even further if necessary to meet group needs by simply having people state their name when the music stops. Many other topics can also be added if required. Using the music adds an extra pleasant stimulant to help arouse people and prepare them for other activities.

Tea Party

Materials

None.

Preparation

Prepare in advance a list of topics such as the following:

* Why I have come here today.
* What I would be doing if I were not here now.
* What I would most like to do in all the world.
* The famous person I would most like to meet.
* My last holiday.

Procedure

Have the group form an inner and outer circle so that each person in the inner group is facing someone in the outer circle – a partner. Partners can have chairs to sit on if this is desirable. The group leader calls out a topic from the prepared list and partners have a quick conversation about it. At the end of a minute, the group leader calls out 'Change'. Either the inner or the outer circle gets up and moves round one chair to their left. When everyone is facing a new partner, the group leader announces a new topic. Every minute, 'Change' is called and the exercise is repeated, until everyone has met everyone else or there is a natural end.

Variation

Give each group member a prepared list of appropriate questions on a handout; for example:

* What do you enjoy doing in your leisure time?
* Why do you come to this group?
* What do you like best about the centre/home?
* What do you dislike most about the centre/home?

Ask them to form into pairs and give them a moment or two to talk to each other finding out the answers to the questions. Signal for each person to find a new partner by calling out, 'Change'. Continue doing this until everyone has had an opportunity to meet everyone else.

Comment

Giving participants a list of questions to ask can help them progress beyond asking safe questions about names, jobs, workplace and so on. Thus, with a group who know each other slightly, carefully prepared questions and topics can lead them to develop relationships on a deeper level. If group members are unfamiliar with each other, you can progress from one level to another. This noisy game is called 'Tea Party' as it derives from the Mad Hatter's tea party in Lewis Carroll's *Alice in Wonderland*.

Friendly Greetings

Materials

Some cards and a pen.

Preparation

Prepare a set of cards, each of which has a greeting of some sort written on it which has to be said or performed. Examples:

✱ 'Hello, how are you, Joyce?'
✱ Shake hands with Paul and say, 'Pleased to meet you, Paul.'
✱ 'Hello Bob, do you like this warm weather?'
✱ Bow to Carol and say, 'Are you warm enough, Carol?'
✱ 'Did you sleep well last night, Pat?'
✱ 'Did you enjoy your lunch, Ivy?'
✱ Curtsey to Jean and say, 'Good morning Jean, that is a lovely cardigan you are wearing?'

Ensure that each card has someone's name on it and that the action or greeting is appropriate to each person named. Prepare enough cards for at least two rounds.

Procedure

Have everyone sit in a circle. Explain that the aim of the game is to help people learn each other's names. Players can select a card at random or hand them out. Anyone who gets a card with their own name on it will need to exchange it for another. Ask each person, in turn, to look at the card selected, read it and greet the person named in the fashion indicated. If they do not know who the person is, they will need to ask. Encourage the person greeted to acknowledge the greeting appropriately. Continue in this fashion until all the cards have been used.

Variation

Ask each member of the group, in turn, to speak to the person on their right, stating their name and making a friendly greeting. (Cards can be used for this without the names if you are not sure who will sit next to whom.)

Comment

A friendly greeting invariably brings forth a friendly response and stimulates a warm feeling to start the group. If group abilities allow it, the cards can be dispensed with and everyone can make up their own friendly action and greeting to another group member.

Musical Greetings

Materials

Paper, pen, a bag, music and a machine to play the music on.

Preparation

Write a number of instructions on separate sheets of paper. Examples:

* Say good morning to the person opposite to you.
* Shake hands with the third person on your right.
* Smile, and wave to the fifth person on your left.
* Blow a kiss to a person of the opposite sex.
* Wave with both hands to the person furthest away from you.

Make the greetings as simple, active or daring as appropriate for the group. Place all the pieces of paper in a bag or another suitable container.

Procedure

Have everyone sit in a circle and start the music. Begin passing the bag around from person to person. When the music stops, whoever is holding the bag has to take an instruction out of the bag and do what it says. When that has been completed, start the music again and follow the same procedure. Continue in this manner until all the instructions have been used or everyone has had a greeting addressed to them.

Variation

Instead of using instructions and a bag, use a ball or bean bag to pass from person to person when the music is playing. When the music stops, the person holding the ball says something pleasant to the person on their right.

Comment

This is a delightful game which can ensure that people who may not normally greet each other have the opportunity to do so.

P

SECTION 2
Movement

Games and activities which require some physical effort and bodily responses. The emphasis is on encouraging non-verbal communication and a positive concept of self and the body.

Hand Gestures

Materials

A pen, pieces of paper equal to the number of people in the group and a bag.

Preparation

Write down different meanings – one to a piece of paper – which can be expressed with the hands. Examples:

come on	go away	quiet
praying	I love you	goodbye
listen	go to sleep	shake hands
wash my face	go for a walk	drink a cup of tea
money	play cards	I'm angry
rocking the baby	come here	play tennis

Fold the slips of paper and put them in a bag.

Procedure

Ideally, have everyone sit in a circle. Ask a member of the group to pick one of the pieces of paper out of the bag. The person then demonstrates the gesture with their hands. The rest of the group guesses the meaning. When this has been achieved, ask another volunteer to choose and demonstrate another gesture. Continue until everyone has had a turn. Complete the exercise by having a general discussion on how each person has used their hands during their lifetime.

Variation

Have each group member demonstrate in mime one way in which they have used their hands in the past. Examples might be writing, sewing, woodcarving, washing up, painting, polishing, reading, cutting hair, driving, planting flowers, and so on. As each person will have used their hands for a wide variety of tasks, this can be kept going round the group several times, each person demonstrating something different each time.

Comment

This activity can be adapted for all age groups. It is important to take into account the physical condition of individuals. With the very elderly it need not be performed in a vigorous manner. Also the mime can be performed standing, sitting or lying down, as required. The activity encourages non-verbal communication as well as providing movement.

Going Through the Motions

Materials

None.

Preparation

None.

Procedure

Form the group into a circle. Start the game by performing a movement or having a player think of one. This could be tapping a foot, waving, touching a knee, looking over a shoulder, wriggling fingers, and so on. The player next to you then repeats the movement you performed and adds one of their own. The third player now does the first two actions plus a third. This continues on around the circle until everyone has added a movement.

Variation

It helps players remember the movements, and can be more fun, if all the players who have performed a movement do all the movements together each time. The person whose turn it is adds an additional movement. Eventually, everyone is in motion together.

Comment

Movements can be kept simple, made more complicated or energetic, as required to meet the needs of the group. This is also a good memory exercise.

Moving Target

Materials

A large ball, bean bags or sponges equal to the number of people in the group.

Preparation

None.

Procedure

Have the players form a semi-circle or a straight line and give each person a sponge. Now roll the ball across the floor in a straight line. As the ball rolls group members throw their sponges and try to hit the moving target. Repeat this a number of times.

Variations

1. Roll a hoop of some sort – about two feet (60 cm) in diameter, made from cane or plastic – across the floor. The thrown sponges are aimed to go through the hoop.
2. For really active and able groups, throw the hoop across the space, to be caught by someone on the other side. See how many sponges players can get through the hoop.

Comment

Adjust the speed and size of the ball, the distance between ball and throwers and the subtlety of how it is released to meet the skills and needs of the group members. No one is singled out for missing and everyone is involved in a common aim.

keep the Ball in Motion

Materials

A double sized bedsheet and a large ball.

Preparation

None.

Procedure

Have everyone gather round the sheet and grasp the edges, lifting it to chest height. Throw the ball onto the sheet. The group now try to get the ball to move around the sheet in a circular motion. To achieve this, some members will have to lower their side to get the ball moving while the others lift. Those who lowered their side will have to lift it back up to stop the ball rolling off the edge and back towards the other edge. The aim is to keep the ball moving around in a circle without it going off the edge.

Variation

The group flip their arms upwards so that the sheet balloons upwards. While it is up in the air, one nominated group member lets go, crosses underneath the ballooning sheet to the other side and gets hold of the sheet again. The group continues in this manner until everyone has had a chance to go underneath. Do make sure the ceiling is high enough or perform the exercise outside.

Comment

This is a game which is fun and which takes a little practice to enable the group to keep the ball in motion. Moving under the sheet creates a really nice experience. Once the sheet is ballooned up there is lots of time for the nominated person to move from one side to the other – they do not have to run or hurry.

Freeze

Materials

Music and a machine to play it on.

Preparation

None.

Procedure

Start the music playing. Begin a simple movement to the rhythm of the music or invite a group member to do so. This may be something like clicking the fingers. All the group members now join in until the group leader shouts 'Freeze'. Then the person to the right of the leader starts another movement, this could be conducting with their hands, for example. This continues until 'Freeze' is called again. The next player now starts a third movement, which could be tapping their toes to the rhythm. This continues round the group until everyone has had an opportunity to add a movement.

Variations

1   If the group is able, get them to do a different dance movement each time 'Freeze' is called.
2   Get each member of the group to start a different keep-fit exercise each time 'Freeze' is called.

Comment

This is an enjoyable activity which can be used with all age groups and is easily adapted to abilities.

Floor Dominoes

Materials

A number of A4 size cards and a magic marker.

Preparation

Draw domino symbols on the cards, using dots from one to six as with normal dominoes.

Procedure

Give each group member a card and then begin play using normal domino rules. Each person places their card appropriately on the floor.

Variation

Instead of dots paste pictures cut from magazines onto the cards. Again, as in dominoes, like must be placed next to like: a picture of a child against a picture of another child, and so on. Images, either dots or pictures, must be big enough to be seen from some distance.

Comment

This activity combines bending movement, concentration and attention, eye scan and is good fun.

Touch Game

Materials

None.

Preparation

None.

Procedure

Have group members sit fairly close to each other. Ask each person to 'Touch your knee', 'Put your hands on your waist', 'Hold hands with the person next to you', 'Place a hand on someone's shoulder'. Continue in this manner for a few minutes and then have a pause and see if people can remember who they have held hands with and so on. If appropriate, repeat with a group member calling out the commands.

Variations

1 If the group members are reasonably active, have them touch various items in the room.
2 Use colours. Ask group members to touch something or someone wearing the colour brown, then blue and so on. Also use colours liked, disliked or favoured. This variation can be ended with a brief discussion on favourite coloured clothes, rooms, cars and so on.

Comment

This is an activity which encourages movement and sensory stimulation and which exercises memory skills, while being good fun. It is best to start with people touching parts of their own body first and then to progress to touching others.

 Do be sensitive and ensure that when touching other people, each person is comfortable with this and it is done appropriately.

Orchestral Mime

Materials

Blackboard and chalk or flipchart and magic marker, orchestral music tape, record or CD and a machine to play it.

Preparation

None.

Procedure

Get everyone to call out as many orchestral instruments as they can think of and write them on the flipchart. Think of all the different sections of an orchestra: string, brass, woodwind and percussion. Do not forget the baton. Let people talk about the instruments, likes, dislikes and so on. When enough have been called out, go round the group asking individuals to choose an instrument and mime playing it. When this has been completed, switch on the orchestral music tape and ask everyone to mime together to the music.

Variations

1 Divide the large group into small groups, with each group playing an instrument from a section of the orchestra.
2 Have individuals mime playing an instrument and the other group members guess the instrument.

Comment

While this game is particularly good for young people, it is enjoyable for all ages and encourages movement. The activity can be done sitting or, if abilities permit, you could get people to stand up when miming.

Follow the Leader

Materials

Music and a machine to play it on.

Preparation

None.

Procedure

Ensure that each person is sitting or standing at least two arm's lengths apart. Tell the group that they must do what you do, following your every movement. Start the music playing and begin making movements in time with the music. Raise your right hand slowly, then your left hand. Lower your right hand and then your left hand. Glance to the right, then to the left. Continue creating movements in this manner, going slowly until the group members have got the idea and then speeding up appropriately. You can include many different movements to suit any type of group and ability. Other types of movement could include brushing teeth, combing hair, having a cup of tea, putting on make-up, washing and so on.

Variation

Divide the group into pairs. Have partners face each other. First one person can lead the movements and the other can follow. After a short period, change over, so that the other person takes the lead.

Comment

This is a delightful activity which allows you to direct movement to all parts of the body in a gentle and enjoyable manner.

Action Story

Materials

Music and a machine to play it on.

Preparation

Write down a storyline or a list of actions and qualifiers. Examples:

running	skipping	slowly
jumping	hopping	drunkenly
riding	tiptoeing	happily
flying	sideways	proudly
dancing	skating	hurriedly
backwards	limping	lazily

Procedure

Stand in the centre of the room where everyone can see and hear you. Have music playing in the background. Start everyone walking freely round the room and invent an action story which connects the movements. Here is an example:

'Tom walked slowly through the forest. Dawn was breaking. Suddenly, he heard a noise. A twig snapped. He stopped. What was it? A predator in the forest. Tom walked on hurriedly. He heard it again. Panicking, he ran and ran and ran until he came to a river. The sound behind was coming nearer, and getting louder. He jumped into the river and began to swim hurriedly towards the other side ...'

And so on. The players act out the story and perform the actions as the story is told. There is no need to keep the story line logical, but do try to create atmosphere with tone of voice. It is helpful to write down some sort of story line or a list of actions, so that the movements can be kept going easily.

Variations

1 Start the story line off. After a moment or two, have a group member continue it. Continue changing the narrator every couple of minutes until everyone has had a turn.

2 Start everyone walking round the room. After a lap or two, ask them to mime swimming around the room. Continue in this manner, changing the ways of moving around the room every few laps.

Comment

This is a game which can be used with people of all ages. The actions can be varied to suit. Less able people can do simple actions seated in their chairs, if necessary. The activity, especially in story form, will still be very enjoyable and stimulating.

Blowing in the Wind

Materials

A ping-pong ball and a small piece of material about three to four foot (1 metre) square. Two or three pieces of material and ping-pong balls may be needed for larger groups.

Preparation

None.

Procedure

Divide the participants into small groups, with individuals sitting opposite each other. Arrange people so that they can hold the material up to neck level. Now place a ping-pong ball in the centre of the piece of material and ask players to blow the ball across to the player opposite. He or she, in turn, blows the ball back. See how long groups can keep the ball in play without it falling off the material.

Variation

Instead of a piece of material, use a table with everyone seated around it.

Comment

This game provides good breathing exercise as well as being an excellent means of releasing tension.

> ⚠ **However, do be aware that taking too many deep breaths in too short a time can cause dizziness or hyperventilation.**

Photo Posing

Materials

Two chairs, pieces of paper and a bag.

Preparation

Think up a selection of situations or activities such as:

working in a shop	cycling	skiing
ballroom dancing	climbing	sailing
a christening	on holiday	playing football
on honeymoon	getting married	playing hockey

Write each situation or activity on a slip of paper and put them in a bag.

Procedure

Form the group into a circle and place two chairs in the centre. Ask for two volunteers. Now another group member picks a situation from the bag and poses the two volunteers in a manner which demonstrates, as in a photograph, the situation or activity chosen. The two chairs can be used as props to assist the pose. When the picture is complete, the person arranging it steps back and pretends to take a photograph. The other group members now have to guess the theme, situation or activity. When it has been guessed, the photographer takes the place of one of the volunteers. Another person is invited to pick a theme from the bag and the procedure begins again.

P

Variations

1 Use abstract themes, such as joy, kindness, apathy, obedience, love, anger, laziness and so on.
2 Have two participants act out a chosen scene in silence as in a silent movie.

Comment

This activity allows physical contact in an acceptable manner, as well as providing some physical movement. It also enables players to use creative abilities. Do bear in mind that situations or activities are much easier to pose for than abstract themes.

In the Manner of ...

Materials

Pieces of paper and a bag.

Preparation

Write the name of an animal on each piece of paper and place them in a bag: for example, penguin, ape, duck, hen, kangaroo, rabbit, pigeon, cat, dog, and so on.

Procedure

Each person in the group draws out a piece of paper from the bag. After allowing a moment for thought, ask for a volunteer to go into the centre of the group and mime being the animal they have chosen. They could walk in the manner of the penguin, do head movements in the manner of a hen, and so on. The group tries to guess which animal is being mimed. If people are having difficulty guessing the animal, invite the person miming to add sound to their demonstration. This should enable the animal to be easily guessed.

Variation

Call out the name of an animal or bird. Everybody walks round the room miming both the walk and the sound for a moment or two. Then a group member calls out another animal which everybody mimes.

Comment

Having everyone do the mime together avoids anyone feeling silly. It is also really good fun, as most people cannot do it without breaking out into laughter.

What I Would Like to See

Materials

None.

Preparation

None.

Procedure

Have everyone close their eyes and cup their hands over them. Ask them to relax and to be aware of how they feel and what they see (with hands still over their eyes). Next, ask them what they would like to see and what they wish to avoid seeing. Finally, ask them what they can see better with their eyes closed. Allow a few moments for people to think and then ask them to open their eyes again. Now have a discussion about each task you have asked them to do.

Variations

1 Follow the same procedure for hearing.
2 Follow the same procedure for smelling. People can pinch their noses, but do make sure everyone is breathing comfortably through their mouths.
3 Touch can be added by having everyone close their eyes and imagining themselves touching various things, or being touched.
4 For taste, it is helpful to have everyone close their eyes and imagine what they can taste now, what they like to taste and what tastes they like to avoid.

Comment

A very useful exercise, this covers all the senses and brings out the most surprising things. It also stimulates humour.

Change Partners

Materials

A record, tape or CD which is good for dancing, and a machine to play it on.

Preparation

None.

Procedure

Divide the group into pairs, or have each person choose a partner. Start the music and invite everyone to start dancing with their partner. After a couple of moments, call out 'Change partners'. Everyone now leaves their partner and chooses someone new to dance with. Continue in this manner until everyone has had an opportunity to dance with everyone else.

Variation

The group leader chooses a partner and begins dancing to the music. On the call 'Change partners', both dancers choose another partner from the group to dance with. On the next call, 'Change partners', the four people dancing choose new partners from those not dancing. Continue until everyone is dancing. This works well with a very large group.

Comment

This works well with all age groups. Explain that people do not have to do a formal dance but can choose simply to move or sway to the music. This way the dancing can be as gentle or as exuberant as necessary to suit the group.

Balloons

Materials

Balloons and music.

Preparation

None.

Procedure

Split the group into pairs. Give each pair a blown-up balloon. Invite the partners to keep the balloons airborne using their joint efforts, and start the music playing. Every few minutes, stop the music. This is a signal for everyone to change partners. The new partners now keep a balloon airborne until the music stops again. Continue in this manner for as long as is appropriate.

Variation

Have a balloon which the whole group must keep airborne, patting it from one to another. See how long it can be kept airborne.

Comment

To provide good breathing practice, give each member of the group a balloon to blow up. When the balloons have been inflated, proceed to the activity. This is another good activity for releasing tension.

Five Up

Materials

None.

Preparation

None.

Procedure

Ensure that everyone is sitting. Explain that the idea is that five people should always be standing but no one can remain standing for more than five to ten seconds at a time before they sit down again. Once sat down, they can get straight up again if they wish. Anyone can stand up when they want. The aim is to have five people standing all the time.

Variation

Instead of starting with each person sitting, reverse this and begin with everyone standing. The aim, of course, will be to have five people sitting all the time.

Comment

This is a silly but hilarious game. It is a good game to use to energize people when things are getting dull. As it is non-threatening, it is a useful game to play with people who are resistant to playing together. You can reduce or increase the number of people required to be standing or sitting at any time during the game.

Favourite Exercises

Materials

Flipchart and magic marker.

Preparation

None.

Procedure

Ask each group member to think of a favourite exercise which they enjoy and which makes them feel good. This may be stretching, having a good yawn, an arm or leg exercise, deep breathing, a wrist exercise or whatever else they like. Now ask for a member to volunteer and lead the group in the exercise of their choice. When this has been completed, have another person demonstrate their favourite exercise, which everybody joins them in performing. Continue in this manner until everyone has had an opportunity to do their own favourite exercise.

Variation

Have people call out exercises they enjoy doing. Write each one up on a flipchart, using a magic marker. Next have everyone do all the exercises listed, one by one.

Comment

This is always a success. The fun is enjoyed by everyone and all feel they have contributed to the activity.

Musical Exercises

Materials

Music and a machine to play it.

Preparation

None.

Procedure

Make sure each person is sitting or standing far enough apart to not touch each other with their arms outstretched. Start the music playing and begin the warming-up process by having everyone swaying and moving to the rhythm of the music.

After a few moments, get each person to rub their hands together. Next, have them start to gently slap themselves all over their bodies. Now move on to participants moving their heads up and down in a nodding motion, then swivelling the head to the left and right. Next, everyone shrugs their shoulders up and down a few times, following this with a circular motion, first with the left shoulder and then the right. Proceed to swinging the hips from side to side, then stretching the trunk forwards, backwards and sideways.

Those who are standing doing the exercises can go down to a squatting position and up again. If sitting, members can stretch their legs out, pointing their toes to the centre of the circle and then gently circling the feet from the ankle. It may be easier for some people to do this one leg at a time.

Now have everyone stretch upwards, reaching to touch the ceiling and down again. Finish by swaying or moving the body to the rhythm of the music again. Repeat as appropriate.

Variation

For more able groups, you may wish to introduce some floor exercises: lying on the back doing cycling motions, scissor movements and so on.

Comment

The music can be fast or slow and the exercises can be performed gently or vigorously to suit the requirements of the group. You can also introduce other exercises, more gentle or strenuous, as required.

Tense and Relax

Materials

None.

Preparation

None.

Procedure

Ensure that each person is sitting in a comfortable chair with good back support. Instruct everyone to adapt a passive ('Let it happen') attitude. Explain that the idea is to tense a group of muscles, concentrate on the feeling of strain for a few seconds and then relax them. The exercise involves doing this for all parts of the body. Each person breathes slowly and regularly between stages and during each stage. When everyone is ready, talk them through the following stages:

1. **Feet:** pull your toes upwards and tense your feet muscles. Hold, relax and repeat.

2. **Legs:** lift your legs off the floor, straighten them out and bring your toes back towards your face. Hold, relax and repeat. Now point your toes forward and down. Hold, relax and repeat.

3. **Abdomen:** pull your stomach muscles in and tense. Hold, relax and repeat.

4. **Back:** arch and tense your back. Hold, relax and repeat.

5. **Shoulders and neck:** bring your shoulders up towards your ears and tense. Hold, relax and repeat. Press your head back and tense. Hold, relax and repeat.

6. **Arms:** stretch out your arms and hands as far as you can, attempting to touch the walls on each side of the room, and tense. Hold, relax and repeat.

7. **Face:** tense your face by lowering the eyebrows, biting hard and screwing

up your face. Hold, relax and repeat.

8 **The whole body:** clench your fists, hold your arms in close to your body, press your knees together and tense your whole body. Hold, relax and repeat.

9 **The mind:** now spend a few minutes relaxing your mind. Close your eyes and think about something restful and pleasant, a scene or image which works best for you.

Give participants time to contemplate their relaxing scene, then ask them to open their eyes, stretch gently and move about in their seat. Finish the exercise by asking everyone, in turn, how it went for them.

Variation

Go through each muscle group, but this time have everyone loosely flex each group of muscles: doing a circling motion with each foot, shaking each leg in a loose manner, doing a circular motion or wriggling the hips, flexing the shoulders, shaking the arms and hands loosely and doing a gentle circular motion with the head.

Comment

These are efficient tension relievers which make people feel good afterwards.

SECTION 3

Perception

Games which provide sensory stimulation and promote awareness of the physical world as well as memory and emotional associations. The activities can be used to aid sensory deprivation, poor attention span and sensory diminishment.

Simon Says

Materials

None.

Preparation

None.

Procedure

This game can be performed with the players seated or standing. Either the group leader or a group member gives the commands. This person calls out: 'Simon says "Bend your left elbow".' Everyone then carries out the action. The next command might be 'Touch your right knee', 'Shrug your right shoulder', 'Move your left foot' or 'Open your mouth'.

Normally, when playing this game, if an order is given without the prefix 'Simon says', anyone completing the movement is out of the game. To avoid this competitive element, instead of eliminating the person who completes the action from the game, have them call out the next series of commands until someone else completes the movement without the prefix. Alternatively, when starting the game, split the group into two or three teams. Anyone who completes an action without the prefix 'Simon says' then changes to another team. Players changing teams then become part of the fun.

Variation

'Do this, do that': the rules are the same as for 'Simon says', except that the leader says 'Do this' or 'Do that'. Players do the action when 'Do this' is called out and refrain from doing it on the command 'Do that'.

Comment

This is an excellent body image activity. The pace can be adapted to suit individual abilities. It will also aid quick thinking and concentration, and promote movement.

I Spy

Materials

None.

Preparation

None.

Procedure

Encourage everyone to sit in a circle. Invite someone to start the game by completing the 'I spy ...' sentence. When completing the sentence, they must refer to the shape of the object in mind. They could say 'I spy something which is round.' Everyone then tries to guess what it is the person means. When it has been guessed, another player has a go. He may say, 'I spy something which is a rectangular shape.' Proceed in this manner until everyone has had a go completing the 'I spy ...' sentence and the object referred to has been guessed.

Variations

1 Instead of shape use colour: 'I spy something that is red.'
2 Use size: 'I spy something that is about 12 inches long and one inch wide.'
3 Have a round using shape, then colour and lastly size.

Comment

If 'I spy ...' might appear childish to people substitute the words, 'I'm thinking of something in the room which is ...'

P

Guess the Smell

Materials

Jam jars, materials to smell, paper and pencil.

Preparation

Put a number of strong-smelling items into the jars, which have been wrapped with paper or cloth, numbered and had holes pricked in the metal tops. The items or substances can be vinegar, lemon, mustard, vanilla, perfume, jam or whatever else you please.

Procedure

Pass the jars round, one at a time, to each member of the group. Individuals smell the jars and write down whatever they think is in them. When everyone has had a chance to smell all the jars, ask group members to call out what they think was in each jar, starting with jar number one. Pass the jars round again so that those who are doubtful can confirm what it is. The emphasis is on identifying the smell, not on how many each person has got right.

Variation

Pass one jar round and have group members call out what they think is in it after it has been circulated. When it has been successfully identified and everyone has had an opportunity to confirm the smell, go on to the next jar.

Comment

Allow plenty of time for identification of the smell and encourage the stimulation of memories associated with them.

Picture Puzzles

Materials

A large sheet of paper or a poster and magic markers.

Preparation

Obtain a large poster or draw a large picture with a number of figures, objects or shapes on it. The picture should be about three or four feet square. Using chalk, draw a rectangle or square on the floor the same size as the poster. Cut the poster up into pieces: these can be a combination of shapes – squares, triangles, curved pieces and so on. The size of the pieces and the configuration of the shapes will need to be chosen to suit the abilities of the group members. It may be necessary to 'grade' the pieces from simple to more complicated to allow for individual abilities.

Procedure

Hand out the pieces of the picture to group members. Ask participants, one at a time, to place their pieces in the square. Encourage players to work together and help each other. As members see that a piece they have fits they can place it in the frame. Continue in this manner until the picture is complete. Once it is finished, give participants time to look at the picture and have them name objects in it.

Variation

Draw large human figures of a man and a woman (have two volunteers lie on a large sheet of paper and draw round their silhouettes). When the figures are complete, cut them into large sections: for example, hands, feet, legs, torso and so on. Now give the pieces out to individuals and see if they can construct the figures. As players place their pieces, have them state what it is: hand, foot and so on.

Comment

Do ensure that participants stand round the drawn square and bend down to place the pieces, thus using motor planning movements, and encourage them to work co-operatively as a group. The variation can be used with group members who have more severe problems.

Taste Test

Materials

Drinking glasses. An assortment of drinks, blindfolds and a screen of some sort.

Preparation

None.

Procedure

Blindfold each person in turn, lead them behind the screen and give them a sip from a prepared glass. The person blindfolded is led back to their place and the blindfold removed. Ensure that participants do not say what they think the drink was while waiting for the others to have a taste. When all have had a sip, ask what it was they thought they had tasted. You can have members shout this out or give one person the opportunity to make a first guess and see if the others agree. Continue in this manner until all the different drinks have been identified.

Variation

Instead of drinks, use food such as jams, different types of cake, vegetables, fruit or meats.

Comment

This activity usually generates good interaction as well as activating the sense of taste. There will also be many different reactions, including the stimulation of memories.

> ⚠ **Do make yourself aware of what is acceptable and safe for each group member to eat and drink when preparing for this exercise.**

It is also inadvisable to use anything that is bitter or could be unpleasant to taste.

If anyone is apprehensive about using a blindfold, simply ask them to keep their eyes closed when behind the screen.

Describing Game

Materials

Pencils, paper and a selection of objects to draw such as a paperweight, a book, a stapler and a bulldog clip.

Preparation

None.

Procedure

Ask participants to elect a partner. Have them decide which one is to be known as A and which B. Next, seat them in rows so that the As are seated with their backs to the Bs. Hand the A players a pencil and a sheet of drawing paper each. Then, without the As seeing, give each of the Bs a different object. The person with the object now describes it in terms of size, shape, texture and so on, so that their partner can draw it without seeing it. The person describing the object must not say what it is.

When the drawing is complete, or an allotted time is up, collect the objects again, still not showing them to the As. The Bs are handed pencils and paper and the As given objects to be described and drawn by the Bs. When this has been completed, the objects are again collected up.

Everyone is now seated in a circle and all the objects are placed in the centre. One by one, each of the players holds up their drawing and tries to pick out the object it represents. If they fail, have other players assist them. The person who described the object confirms it is the right one or, as a last source of identification, states the correct object.

P

Variation

1. Instead of objects have a selection of pictures of different types of animals, birds and fish. Again participants describe the shape without saying what it is.

2. Give one player an object in a bag behind their back. They are only allowed to feel the object as they attempt to describe it. The other group members have to try to guess what it is from the description. Ensure that every player has a go at describing an object.

Comment

This is a good game for encouraging interaction and perception of shapes.

Identify the Sound

Materials

A curtain or bedsheet and instruments to make sounds.

Preparation

Hang the curtain or sheet up so that one or two people can be hidden behind it to make the sounds. Alternatively, sounds can be recorded but this is not as much fun as actually making the sounds. Make sure that all the instruments are handy to make the sounds, which might include the following:

striking a match	pouring water
using a food mixer	beating an egg
different musical instruments	making tea
sawing	hammering a nail

vacuuming

Procedure

Once all is set, start the first sound. You can have people shout out what they think it is or give each person an opportunity to be first to have a guess at the sound. If they have difficulty identifying it, give the rest of the group a chance to help them out. Encourage discussion about the sounds and any memories that are evoked.

Variations

1 Have a discussion on the theme, 'Sounds in my life' or 'Sounds from the past'. Get each person to state a sound in the chosen category. Have them explain the sound, describe it and the memories it evokes. Also get them to imitate it.

2 Record the voices of famous people from the television or the radio. Get participants to identify them. Ensure that players have an opportunity to comment about the person. Do they like or dislike them?

Comment

There are recorded sounds available from Speechmark. These are very useful, particularly for outside sounds such as traffic, trains and so on. You can always use a mixture of created and recorded sounds.

Emotional Headbands

Materials

Pen, paper and string to make headbands.

Preparation

Using the paper and string prepare sufficient headbands for all the people in the group. Write a different feeling or emotion on each headband. For example:

⬤ **anger** ⬤

⬤ **amusement** ⬤

⬤ **embarrassment** ⬤

⬤ **hatred** ⬤

contempt

terror

indifference

pleasure

fear

shame

astonishment

joy

Procedure

Tie a headband on each person's head, without letting them see what is written on it. Now get everyone to move around and react to each person they meet in the manner of the feeling or emotion written on the headband of the person they are approaching. This must be done without speaking. After five minutes or so have everyone sit in a circle and ask each person (a) what they think is written on their headband, and (b) what made them think what they did. Confirm if they thought correctly by having them take off their headband to check.

Variation

Have players approach each other as above, but this time they must speak in the manner of the word written on the other person's headband.

Comment

This is a good emotional perception game which can be a lot of fun.

P

Drama

Materials

Blackboard and chalk or a flipchart and magic marker. Some background music.

Preparation

Have a theme in mind, such as going on holiday, laying out a garden, going shopping, preparing a meal and so on.

Procedure

Having decided on a theme, get the group members to call out everything that needs to be done to complete the task. Write these all up on the flipchart. If you were laying out a garden, this might include digging the ground, cutting the grass, pulling out weeds, levelling the ground, sowing seeds, planting borders, pruning the shrubs, and so on. Once all the tasks have been written down, start the music and call out all the actions one by one. All the group members mime doing the actions until the garden is complete. End with a short discussion on the theme – in this case gardening. Who likes gardening? Who hates it? Are there any famous or local gardens people have visited?

Variation

To choose a theme, invite group members to suggest things they have done in the past. This might be a job, a hobby, or an achievement like winning a race or climbing a mountain. Choose one theme and follow the procedure as above. If a lot of themes have been suggested, do one theme each time the group meets until all have been mimed.

Comment

The themes and acting them out will stimulate memories for the discussion and aid interaction. The dramas can be made simple or more complex to suit the needs of the group.

Loss

Materials

A flipchart and magic marker.

Preparation

None.

Procedure

Invite all the participants to call out losses we experience in life. As they are called out write them up on the flipchart. Many things involve loss, including the following:

moving house	**redundancy**
retirement	**getting married**
leaving home	**something stolen**
something mislaid	**time for self**
physical contact	**stimulating conversation**
a partner	**friendship**
divorce	**youth**
a lifestyle	**changing jobs**
a favourite object	**use of a car**

Groups will come up with dozens of types of loss. When the flipchart page is full ask group members, one at a time, to choose a loss they have experienced and share it with the group. It must be a loss that each person feels comfortable sharing. A large number of losses will involve good things that have happened to people. For example, when someone moves to a better job they may feel the loss of supportive colleagues or lose contact with familiar friends.

It can be very helpful to close the activity with a discussion on how each person likes to be treated when dealing with a loss. Some will like to talk about it, some to be held or hugged, others will like to be left alone but to know someone is nearby if needed.

Variation

Have each person write down a short list of some of the losses they have experienced. Next split a larger group into small groups of three or four people, so they can talk about their losses.

Comment

People seldom get an opportunity to talk about their losses – too often this is avoided, frequently because of the group leader's needless fear of it.

How I see Myself

Materials

Pens, paper and a bag.

Preparation

None.

Procedure

Give each person a pen and a sheet of paper. Ask them to imagine that they are going to meet a complete stranger who is arriving at the local station by train. They have never seen this person before. This person is themselves. Ask them to write a description of this person. Allow five to ten minutes, depending on group abilities. Help anyone who needs assistance. When they are completed, collect up the sheets of paper, fold them and put them in a bag. Have one sheet picked out at a time and read out. See if the group can identify who is being described. When the person is identified, encourage comments which help to correct perceptions that are not accurate.

Variations

1 Have each group member describe someone else in the group in the same manner.
2 Ask each person, in turn, to describe someone else in the group verbally, without referring to their clothes. The group must guess who it is.

Comment

This is a good self-awareness exercise which is also fun.

My Support System

Materials

Large sheets of paper, glue, scissors and lots of magazines.

Preparation

None.

Procedure

Seat everyone around tables with plenty of space. Request that each person look through the magazines and cut out a picture which they feel represents themselves and glue it in the middle of their sheet of paper. Now ask them to think of people to whom they turn when they are happy, lonely or confused, for conversation, entertainment, company and so on. Request that they look through the magazines again and cut out people to represent these different people in their lives. They then glue them onto their sheet of paper, with the people they feel are closest to them nearest to the figure representing themselves. When this has been completed, give each person an opportunity to hold up their collage, explain and talk about it. Ask them if there are any changes they would like to make to it? Would they like any of the people to move away further from them or to be closer?

Variations

1. Have participants draw themselves and then the people around them.
2. Ask a group member to stand or sit in the middle of the room. That person then instructs other group members to stand in a position to represent the person's support system. When complete, ask the person to make any changes they feel they would like to make.

Comment

A powerful exercise, this shows each person's perception of their support system.

What am I Feeling?

Materials

Magazines, scissors, pens and paper.

Preparation

Cut out from the magazines a number of pictures of people expressing a wide range of emotions, such as anger, disgust, love, concern, anxiety, joy, surprise and so on. Number each picture clearly.

Procedure

Place the pictures on tables around the room and give each person a pen and a sheet of paper. Have them walk around and write down the emotion they think is being expressed in each picture. When this has been completed, have everyone sit in a circle, then hold up the first picture and invite everyone to say what emotion they think is being expressed. Encourage discussion concerning what it is about the person in the picture – expression, body language – which indicates what individuals perceive. There will be many variations in perceptions. Continue through all the pictures in this manner.

Variation

Instead of having each group member write down the various emotions, hold each picture up in turn, or pass them around, one at a time. Ensure that each person has had a good chance to see it. Now ask everyone to state what emotion they think is being expressed and discuss.

Comment

This is a good exercise which can highlight the differences in the way each person perceives and reads emotions.

Mystery Objects

Materials

A selection of small objects and a bag.

Preparation

Either collect together a selection of small objects or ask group members to bring in one or two objects each from their home. Whichever method you use, collect the objects together before the group starts so no one can see objects they have not provided.

Procedure

Put one of the objects in a bag without revealing what it is. Give the bag to a group member who reaches into the bag and feels the object. Other group members now ask questions about the object, such as the following:

* How does it feel?
* What shape is it?
* Is it hard?
* Is it soft?
* Does it feel smooth?
* Is it flexible?

The group can go on asking questions until they guess what it is. When they do, put another object in the bag and have another volunteer feel inside and answer the questions. Continue in this manner as long as is appropriate or until all the objects have been used. For added difficulty, you can of course have people put their hands in the bag behind their backs.

Variation

Put an object in a bag and tie the neck. Now pass the bag around the group. When everyone has had a chance to feel the object through the bag, invite them to state what they think it is.

Comment

This is a good sensory awareness exercise which encourages social interaction and is good fun. Do ensure that the objects are not easily broken, especially if they belong to group members and may have sentimental value.

Treasured Possessions

Materials

Magic markers and paper.

Preparation

None.

Procedure

Ask the group members to imagine that for some reason – fire or flood – they have to leave their home in a hurry. There is only time to take a few items in a small case. What items would they choose? When everyone has had an opportunity to think, invite a volunteer to share the contents of their imaginary bag with the group. Explore the reasons why they chose the items. Ensure that everyone in the group has an opportunity to share the contents of their bag.

Variation

1 Ask group members to imagine they are going to live on a desert island for the rest of their lives. If they were only allowed to take five objects with them, what would these objects be?
2 Give participants a magic marker and some paper and have them draw the items. When the task is complete, each person in turn shows their items to the group and discusses them.

Comment

A good self-awareness exercise, this stimulates memories and leads to lots of discussion. It is also surprisingly revealing as to what people treasure.

Pass the Object

Materials

A sponge, small ball or other small, soft object.

Preparation

None.

Procedure

Group members sit in a circle. Have one person volunteer to sit in the centre of the group. Ensure that the people in the circle are fairly close together so that they can pass the object from one person to another behind their backs without difficulty. The person in the middle closes their eyes and the others start passing the object round the circle behind their backs. When ready, the person in the middle shouts 'Stop!' and opens their eyes. The person holding the ball tries to conceal this and the person in the middle attempts to guess who has it. If they are correct, the players change places and the process starts again. If wrong, they close their eyes again and have another go. You can limit the number of attempts, if you think it is necessary, before asking another person to volunteer to be in the middle. People usually guess correctly after two or three attempts.

Variations

1   Thread a ring onto some string which is long enough to stretch around the group when sat in a circle. Tie the ends of the string together. One person sits in the middle with eyes closed. The group members hold the string and pass the ring from person to person on the string concealing it in the palms of their hands. When the person in the middle shouts 'Stop!' and opens their eyes, the person with the ring tries to conceal it. The objective is for the person in the middle to guess who has the ring. When they do, players exchange places.

2 Ask everyone in the circle to join hands and explain that a squeeze has to be passed round. Name a person to squeeze the hand of the person on their right. That person then squeezes the hand of the next person and so on round the circle. The person in the middle shouts 'Stop!', opens their eyes, and tries to guess who was the last person to have their hand squeezed. When they guess correctly, the players changes places.

Comment

Ensure that players change the direction, left or right, in which the object is being passed from time to time. This activity can help with awareness of direction. On a purely fun level it never fails.

P

Blind Walk

Materials

Blindfolds.

Preparation

Ensure that there is nothing in the room which people could trip over, or which will hurt anyone if they bump into it.

Procedure

Ask people to choose a partner. One partner puts on a blindfold. All the blindfolded people now begin walking round the room in any direction they want, holding onto the arm or hand of their partner. The person with their eyes open merely helps them keep balance and ensures that they do not blunder into anything that might hurt them. Otherwise, they remain silent and follow the guidance of the blindfolded person. The blindfolded person feels any furniture, materials or objects they come into contact with, and makes themselves aware of any sounds or changes in light they encounter. This continues for about three to five minutes. Then ask everyone to stop. Before removing the blindfolds have everyone state, one at a time, where they think they are in the room. Now have them remove the blindfolds.

The other partners are now blindfolded and go through the same procedure. When both walks have been completed, get everyone together in a circle and have a discussion about what emotions they experienced, what the objects they touched felt like and of what sounds, smells and sensations they became aware. What did it feel like to be supported? What did it feel like to be responsible for the other person? Which role did they prefer?

Variations

1 Taking turns, participants stand their partners at one end of the room and ask them to look at a particular spot in the room. The blindfold is then put on and the person walks towards the chosen spot and stops when they think they have arrived. The blindfold is then removed. The roles are then reversed. When everyone has had a go, have a discussion about how the experience felt.

2 In this variation, one of the partners is blindfolded and the other person guides them around the room by use of voice only. They are only allowed to touch in an emergency. Round off the exercise with a discussion about the experience.

Comment

This exercise stimulates all the senses and perception of direction. It is also surprisingly enjoyable for most people. Lead up to variation 2, the most difficult, by completing the others first. If anyone is apprehensive about using a blindfold, ask them to keep their eyes closed when doing the exercise.

Coloured Emotions

Materials

Flipchart and magic marker.

Preparation

Have about six feelings or emotions in mind, such as happiness, sadness, anger, frustration, warmth and friendliness.

Procedure

Write an emotion up on the flipchart and ask each member of the group to think about what colour they associate with it in their minds. After a pause for thought, ask each person, in turn, to state the colour. When this is completed, encourage open discussion, with the individuals explaining why they chose the colour. Are their feelings about the colour influenced by memories or experiences? What are those memories or experiences? Once one emotion has been exhausted, write another up on the flipchart and continue in the same manner, exploring as many emotions as is appropriate.

Variation

1 Write a colour up on the flipchart and then ask members to state an emotion they associate with it.
2 Have a discussion about favourite or hated colours and why they are liked or disliked.

Comment

It is always best to start and end with a good or positive emotion. This ensures an uplifting end to the exercise.

Through a Window

Materials

Paper, pencils and/or paint.

Preparation

None.

Procedure

Make sure everyone is sitting comfortably. Ask them to close their eyes, relax and imagine themselves looking out of a window. The window can be anywhere they please, imaginary, from memory, or something they would like to see. Ask them to take a good look through the window for a few moments and memorise what they see. After a pause, have participants gently open their eyes and make themselves aware of the room again. Give a moment for everyone to reorient themselves and then have volunteers describe what they saw through their window.

Variations

1   Ask participants to imagine they are on the outside looking in through a window. What do they see?
2   Ask group members to draw what they see. When everyone has completed their drawing, have them held up, one at a time, and commented on by the person who drew it.

Comment

This is a good self-awareness activity which can stimulate memories and elicit individual perspectives on life.

Self-Portraits

Materials

Paper, pencils, crayons.

Preparation

Prepare sheets of paper, divided into three, with the following headings:

How others see me	How I see myself	How I would like to be seen

Procedure

Give each participant a prepared sheet of paper and ask them to draw a picture of themselves under each heading. When this has been completed, give an opportunity for each person to share their perceptions about themselves with the group. Do this by having them hold up their drawings and talk about them to the group. Ensure that the group give each person feedback about their perceptions, particularly concerning the first heading.

Variations

1 Instead of drawing, have each person write a short paragraph expressing their perceptions in each column.
2 Give each person the choice of either drawing or writing their perception.

Comment

Do ensure that the group members feel comfortable and have built up some trust and confidence in each other before doing this exercise.

Cognitive Stimulation

Games which provide problem solving, decision making and creative activity. These are activities which lead to more organized thought.

Pass the Story

Materials

The same number of objects as people in the group.

Preparation

Collect together the objects. These could include a paperweight, an apple, a ruler, a shoe, a piece of rope, a book and so on. The more varied the objects, the better.

Procedure

Have the group members sit in a circle. Place the objects in the centre on a coffee table. Ask participants to choose an object, take it and sit down again. Now either ask a volunteer to begin a story, or do so yourself, including in the opening the object you have chosen. You might begin: 'Peter went into the park and sat down on a bench. He could feel the heat of the sun on his face and smell the freshly cut grass. As he bit into the *apple* he'd brought for lunch, a voice from behind said: "Do you mind if I join you?"' Having started the story and included the object in the narrative, pass the story line on to the next person, who continues with it, including their chosen object in what they say. The story is then passed on to the next player, who proceeds in the same manner. This continues until everyone has had an opportunity to include their object in the story. The last person attempts to bring the story to an end.

Variation

Use pictures cut from magazines. These could be pictures of mountains, streams, woods, a car, a house or a table. Pictures give a much wider scope for what can be included in stories.

Comment

You can add focus and extra interest by stipulating that the story must be comic, a mystery, an adventure, a murder or a romance. Assist each person inventing the story by asking, 'What happened next?', 'What did they do then?' and so on.

I Appreciate ...

Materials

Pieces of paper and pens.

Preparation

None.

Procedure

Give each person a piece of paper and a pen. Ask them to think about things that they appreciate. This might be something that someone does for them, someone's company, a sense of humour, a gift, time on their own and so on. Give a few minutes for everyone to write down three things that they appreciate. (More able groups can write down a greater number and less able groups one thing.) Now ask for a volunteer to read out their list. Encourage the person to say why they appreciate the particular thing. When the first volunteer has finished, ask for someone else to have a go. Continue in this manner until everyone has made a statement.

Variations

There are many variations on this theme. Here are a few:

1. I resent ...
2. I like/dislike ...
3. I am good/bad at ...
4. My biggest problem is ...
5. My greatest joy is ...

Comment

These are really good prompts to encourage discussion creating both self-awareness and awareness of others within the group. For some more able groups you may not want to have participants write their statements. Instead, have them complete the statement verbally. For groups where individuals are more regressed it may be helpful to rephrase the statements as more focussed questions. Examples:

* 'What do I do that you like?'
* 'What does your son do that you appreciate?'
* 'What do you enjoy doing most in the group?'

Poetry Reading

Materials

A selection of poetry books (large-print where appropriate).

Preparation

None.

Procedure

Hand out the poetry books and ask the group members to browse through them and pick out a verse or poem to read. When everyone is ready, ask a volunteer to read their choice out. It is helpful to have them read it out twice, as not everyone will have understood or taken it all in the first time. Now have a brief discussion about the poem. Who liked or disliked it? Relate the poem to feelings, past experience and beliefs of group members. When the discussion has ended, have the poem read out again. This time participants may be able to relate to it better. Next, invite another group member to read their selection out, and so on. If the group is large, this activity can go on for a long time. If appropriate, shorten the time by saying that a particular number of poems will be read out and that the others will be read out when the group next meets.

Variation

Many group members may have written poems of their own or have favourite poems they remember. Invite everyone to bring the poems to the group and share them with each other. It is helpful to liaise with group members before the group starts and have copies of the poems to hand.

Comment

Any activity incorporating poetry will stimulate cognitive and creative processes.

Impromptu Speeches

Materials

Paper, pen, a bag, a flipchart and magic marker.

Preparation

Write a number of topics on pieces of paper and put them in a bag. Examples:

Royalty	**Understanding the opposite sex**
A day by the sea	**School days**
My favourite time of the year	**The cost of living**
How to train a dog	**People I hate**
A day in my life	**My favourite hobby**

Procedure

Seat the participants in a circle and have each take a piece of paper from the bag. Give a moment or two for thought and ask a volunteer to start by giving a one-minute talk on the subject selected. Encourage a light-hearted, amusing approach. When the first person has finished and been applauded, allow some time for discussion and comments on the talk. Afterwards, another player is asked to give their impromptu speech.

Variations

1   To assist less able groups, before each person gives their speech, have a brief brainstorm on the topic, with the whole group, using a flipchart. Write down the suggestions thrown out at random. These can then be used as prompts, if needed, by the person giving the impromptu speech.

2 Introduce the game as 'Nonsense Speeches'. Players talk nonsense about a given topic for one minute. Write appropriate topics on the pieces of paper. Examples:

* Teaching animals to talk
* New uses for old bathtubs
* People who live underwater
* A tasteless invention
* The confessions of a fly.

Comment

This is an exercise which, when embarked on with a sense of fun, promotes good interaction and imaginative thinking.

Monologue

Materials

None.

Preparation

Have in mind a place in which one could be absorbed in private thoughts. Ensure that it is appropriate to group members. Examples:

* a doctor's waiting room
* a bus stop
* the bath
* sitting by the sea

* a train carriage
* an airplane
* a car
* alone in a bedroom

Procedure

Explain that a monologue is only saying your thoughts aloud. Ask group members to think about the given situation and imagine themselves in it: for example, standing at a bus stop. What are they thinking about? What to buy for lunch? Daydreaming about a fantasy holiday or where they would like to be at that moment? Thinking about the family, or what is on TV in the evening? Give a moment for individuals to begin their thoughts and then ask for one member to launch into their monologue, or begin the process yourself. After a minute, the person on your left continues the monologue, picking it up where you have left off. They will likely take it in a completely different direction. This continues round the group until everyone has had an opportunity to add to the monologue.

Variation

Instead of a monologue, begin by starting a story. You can take a story beginning from a book or magazine for this. Each person, in turn, then continues the story, making it up, in the same manner as above. You may wish to stipulate that it is a romantic, crime, science fiction or adventure story before beginning, or just let events take their course.

Comment

Some surprising thoughts can come out of the monologue which give real indications of individuals' thought processes. This aspect can then, if appropriate, become part of a follow up discussion to the exercise. An opportunity is also given for imaginations to have free rein and create really good fun.

Real-Life Events

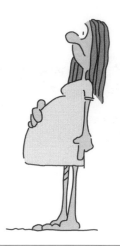

Materials

None.

Preparation

Have in mind a real-life event that has been in the newspapers, a magazine or the news recently. Familiarize yourself with the details about the characters involved and what happened.

Procedure

Have a brief discussion with the group about the real-life event and what happened. Give everyone an opportunity to express their feelings about it. Next, break the large group into smaller groups, each with the same number of people as the number of characters in the event. Ask each group to re-enact the event as in a play, with each person taking a role and presenting their character's viewpoint. If participants find this difficult, have them discuss and argue why their character did what they did. Encourage them to think like the character they are representing. When this phase has been completed, bring everyone back together again and have a final discussion about the event. Has anyone changed the way they felt or thought about the event or the people involved in it?

Variation

Follow the same procedure, but use events taken from soap operas, plays, novels or short stories.

Comment

This is a good way to help participants explore their own and other people's feelings and viewpoints.

> **Do be careful, when choosing material, not to choose events which may be sensitive because of events in members' own lives.**

P

Open Debate

Materials

Two flipcharts and magic markers.

Preparation

Have a topic in mind. This may be something in the news, something from television or an issue which you are aware is important to members of the group. You could also ask group members what they would like to debate. This could include subjects such as whether teachers should be able to punish pupils, drugs should be made legal, the royal family should be abolished, hereditary peers should be able to vote in the House of Lords, cars should be banned from all town centres, and so on.

Procedure

Start the exercise by introducing the topic and asking group members to vote either in favour of or against the proposition to be debated. Do not allow the discussion to begin at this stage – a straightforward 'Yes' or 'No' from participants is all that is required.

Next, label one flipchart 'For' and the other 'Against'. Now have a discussion 'for' the motion and list all the arguments on the appropriate flipchart. When this has been exhausted, switch to 'against' and follow the same procedure.

Ask a group member to summarise each argument, or do this yourself. Finally, have another vote and see if anyone has been persuaded to change their mind. If they have, give them an opportunity to say why.

Variation

Start by voting and then, instead of having an open discussion, divide the group into two. One group is instructed to argue 'for' and the other 'against' the motion. Give each group a flipchart to list their arguments. When sufficient time has elapsed for both groups to prepare their arguments, bring them back together again. Have an elected member from each group present the argument for each side. When both have put their argument, have another vote and see if anyone has changed their mind.

Comment

This activity involves working together, presenting organised thoughts and making decisions. Asking the group members to write down what topics they would like to debate or having a brainstorming session to do this can produce a bank of topics for future debates.

P

Solving a Problem

Materials

Flipchart and magic marker.

Preparation

Have a problem in mind to be solved. This problem will have added interest if it is related to real problems in the day centre, home or hospital in which the group takes place. Examples:

1 Some carers do not understand what we do and why. What can we do about it?
2 What can we do to make the group appeal to more people?
3 We cannot afford more staff to help around the day centre/home. How can we get someone to help out for nothing?
4 We have been given £100 to spend on making this room look better, more comfortable and more appealing. How can we best spend it?
5 What would make the centre/home more welcoming for new people settling in?
6 How could we make better use of the space we have for activities and make it easier for everybody to use?

Procedure

Write the chosen problem up on the flipchart. Give a brief summary of the difficulty explaining why it is a problem. Answer any questions anyone might want to ask to fully understand the situation and invite open discussion. Now ask for possible solutions. No matter how outrageous, write them all up on the flipchart. When the list is complete, look at each suggestion in turn, considering advantages and disadvantages. When all the suggestions have been gone through, have the group decide which suggestion or combination of suggestions will be used to solve the problem. It will then only remain to put the solution into practice.

Variation

Get the group to brainstorm what they see as problems in the centre/home for them as individuals. For example, it may be difficult getting access to rooms or getting information they want. Participants will come up with quite a few matters which can be used for problem-solving sessions.

Comment

It is surprising what comes up in problem-solving sessions. Do not forget that a small group of elderly people will have a few hundred years of experience between them to bring to bear on the problem. When the problems are supplied by participants, you may be astonished by what they see as a problem and has been overlooked or taken for granted. Also the fact that you are using a real problem for the exercise and involving them in the decision making gives it real meaning and will add tremendously to motivation – especially when participants see the solution being put into practice. I have taken to groups problems with which staff have struggled for weeks and been provided with satisfactory solutions.

What Does it Feel Like?

Materials

Some pieces of paper, pens and a bag.

Preparation

Prepare pieces of paper with statements written on them starting with the words 'What does it feel like ...?' For example, what does it feel like

to have a broken leg?	**to be on your own?**
to be a father/mother?	**to be famous?**
to be a truck driver?	**to be in love?**
to be a son/daughter?	**to drive a racing car?**

Procedure

Put all the pieces of paper in a bag or bowl and invite each group member to take one out at random. Give time for participants to think and then ask for a volunteer to read out what is written on their piece of paper. The person then describes what they know or think it feels like. When the person has finished, encourage other group members to comment, adding to what has been said. Some are very likely to have experienced the situation and can give first-hand experience. When the first statement has been exhausted, invite another group member to read from their piece of paper. Continue in this manner until everyone has had an opportunity to take part.

Variation

Instead of using statements written on pieces of paper, use a flipchart. Write a statement on the flipchart and invite group members to respond. When one statement has been exhausted, go on to another. Make sure all group members have an opportunity to respond.

Comment

The questions posed in this exercise lead directly to the use of imagination. The question range should be as wide as possible and include both emotional and humorous questions.

Tell the Truth

Materials

Cards and a pen; a flipchart and magic marker.

Preparation

Prepare cards with a question written on each card. Examples:

If you won £10,000, what would you spend it on?

What frightens you most?

What embarrasses you?

What makes you angry?

If you could choose a famous person to spend an evening with, who would it be?

What makes you laugh?

If you could have anything you wanted, what would it be?

What has annoyed you most during the past week?

What has pleased you most during the past week?

What age would you most like to be?

Procedure

Shuffle the cards and invite each group member to take one. Ask them to read the card. If they would prefer a different card, allow them to choose another from spares you have provided. The group leader also takes a card. When everybody is comfortable with their card, the group leader starts the process by answering the question on the card he or she has chosen. Give the group an opportunity to ask questions and encourage discussion about the answer. When this has been completed, move on to ask another person in the group. Continue in this manner until everyone has had a chance to participate. Do give those who do not want to answer a chance to opt out if they wish, by saying, 'Pass'.

Variation

Write a question on the flipchart and then give all group members in turn a chance to answer the question it. When a question has been exhausted, move on to another.

Comment

Do ensure that the questions are suitable for your particular group and can be answered comfortably, without embarrassment or revealing anything members would prefer to remain unknown.

P

Ship-wrecked

Materials

Drawing paper, pencils, colouring pencils, crayons.

Preparation

Draw the shape of an island on a sheet of paper and photocopy it so each group member can have a copy.

Procedure

Give each group member a sheet of paper with an island drawn on it and a supply of colouring pencils, crayons and so on. Now ask them to imagine themselves shipwrecked on the island. There is no hope of rescue. Request that they draw what they would like to find on the island if they had to spend the rest of their life there. When the task has been completed, get each person to hold their drawing up for the group to see and explain why they have placed what they did on the island. Encourage questions and discussion.

Variation

Draw an island on a flipchart sheet. Invite group members, one at a time, to go up and draw something they would like to find on the island. It can be anything they want. Now discuss why everyone drew what they did.

Comment

As well as stimulating creativity, this exercise ensures group interaction and provides good fun.

What is it?

Materials

A ruler, a ball, a biscuit tin or some other object.

Preparation

None.

Procedure

Show the group the object you have chosen and then demonstrate using it as something else. This may be as a violin, a cricket bat, a back scratcher or whatever else comes to mind. The group members must guess what it is you are using it as. When they have done so, pass the object on to the person next to you. They must now think of something else to demonstrate, for example using it as a tennis racquet. The object is passed around the group in this manner. Each person must think of something new. See how many times it can go round the group without repetition of what has been demonstrated.

Variation

Restrict what is being mimed to musical instruments, sport, hobbies, occupations and so on. Have a round using each heading.

Comment

Once started, people become really imaginative in the way they use the object.

Guess the object

Materials

None.

Preparation

None.

Procedure

Seat the players in a circle and ask for a volunteer to leave the room. While the person is out of the room, the remaining players think of an object. This can be anything – a bed, a potato, a fish, the moon, and so on. Once the object has been decided on, call the volunteer back into the room. This player, by asking each person in the group a question, tries to guess the object. Typical questions might be the following:

* Is it edible?
* Is it manufactured?
* Have you got one?
* Do you use it first thing in the morning?
* Is it round?

The person answering must only say 'Yes' or 'No'. The questions continue until the object is discovered. Another volunteer is then asked to leave the room.

Variations

1   Have one player think of an object and all the other players ask the questions to enable them to guess the answer.
2   Instead of objects, have players think of famous people.

Comment

This is a game which encourages participation and provokes quick thinking.

How Observant are You?

Materials

A large book (such as a biography, a history book or a novel), pen and paper.

Preparation

Write out a list of questions about the book. Examples:

1. What was the title?
2. Who was the author?
3. Who was the publisher?
4. How many pages were there in the book?
5. Was there a dedication?
6. What colour was the cover?
7. Did the book contain illustrations?
8. Was there an introduction?
9. Were the pages numbered at the top or the bottom?
10. How many chapters did the book contain?

Many other questions can be added. The player gets only a glance at the book, so do not ask questions which demand a detailed reading for answers.

Procedure

Seat the players in a circle. Pass the book around the group, giving each person about one minute to examine it. When everyone has had a good look, put the book away somewhere it cannot be seen. Ask the first of the prepared questions and have players shout out the answer. Continue in this manner until all the questions have been answered.

Variation

Follow the same procedure for other types of objects, such as an empty biscuit tin or a picture containing lots of detail.

Comment

This is a good observation and memory game.

P

What I Like When ...

Materials

Flipchart and magic marker or a pen and cards.

Preparation

Think up a list of situations to which the group can relate. Write one situation on each card. For example, 'What I like when ...'

I get up in the morning.	**I'm angry.**
I have my evening meal.	**I get excited.**
I go to bed.	**I'm going out.**
I feel sad.	**I feel happy.**

Procedure

Give each person a card at random. If they do not feel comfortable with the chosen card exchange it for another. Take a card yourself. Start off by disclosing what you like when _____ (whatever is on your card) as an example. Encourage participants to ask questions and discuss your statement. Next, ask a group member to read out what is written on their card and to make their statement. Continue in this manner until everyone has made a statement.

Variation

Instead of cards use a flipchart. Write each statement in turn up on the flipchart and have each group member give their explanation. When one situation has been explored, move on to another.

Comment

This is a good exercise for finding out how participants like situations to be dealt with.

Geographic Circle

Materials

None.

Preparation

None.

Procedure

Have the participants sit in a circle. One player starts by calling out the name of a place. It may be a town, city, county or country, and be anywhere in the world. For example, the first player could call out 'London'. The next person thinks of another place beginning with the last letter of the place previously stated – in this case the letter 'N'. The person might say, 'Nevada'. The next player then says something else beginning with the letter 'A'. And so the game continues round the circle. No player can call out a place previously named: if, for example, the letter 'A' came up several times, players would have to call out a different place each time. See how many times the game can be kept going round the circle.

Variation

Use other categories such as flowers, animals and so on.

Comment

If any player has difficulties, allow the others to help by giving clues, but not actually stating the place to be named.

P

Experience Exchange

Materials

Writing paper and pens.

Preparation

None.

Procedure

Ask group members to think about a good experience that they have had in the past. This may be a holiday, a meeting with old friends, having a meal out, a party, an enjoyable walk and so on. Ask them, one at a time, to recapture the memory by telling the group all about it. This should include how it made them feel and why it was good. Encourage others to share similar experiences.

Variations

1   Have the group members write about their experience and then in turn read out what they have written. Give the whole group an opportunity to comment about each piece and share experiences.

2   Have group members talk or write about:

* an experience they would like to have,
* a bad experience,
* a surprise,
* a frightening experience,
* a happy time,
* anticipating an event which does not happen,
* being in love,
* being alone.

Comment

The variety of experiences is unlimited. If a positive reaction is essential, care should be taken to select the type of subject suitable for the group members. The topics can be used to give an opportunity for individuals to talk about, share and explore experiences they would not normally have a chance to share. If selecting the 'writing' variation, make sure that everyone in the group is able to do this.

Current Affairs

Materials

A variety of different current newspapers.

Preparation

None.

Procedure

Give each person in the group a newspaper, or part of one, and ask them to glance through it, select an item of interest to them or one which they think will interest the group and read it. When everyone is ready, ask for a volunteer to tell the group about the piece they have read. Give time for comments and opinions to be expressed. When this has been completed ask another group member to do the same. Continue in this fashion until everyone has had an opportunity to tell the group about their chosen piece and had it discussed.

Variations

1 Choose one topic from a newspaper and have the group discuss the issue in depth or divide the group into two and debate it.
2 Record a short programme on television concerning a current issue. Play the video – or a short extract from it – back to the group and then discuss or debate the issue.

Comment

Newspapers and issues should be local as well as national. This is a good exercise to use on a regular basis to keep those who are isolated in touch with world events. Also people who live alone or are isolated may not get much opportunity to express and discuss their opinions and ideas about issues.

Ideal Paintings

Materials

Pencils, crayons, paints, water and paper.

Preparation

Ensure that the materials are to hand and that tables or boards are available for participants to work on.

Procedure

Request that participants sketch and paint their ideal room. This may be a room they remember from the past which they particularly liked, how they would like their room to be or a room which they have seen somewhere – perhaps in a magazine, on holiday or when visiting someone. All that is required is quick sketches to present the ideas. When the paintings are completed, have each person in turn hold their painting up and talk about it to the others.

Variations

1   Instead of painting have everyone write a description of their ideal room.
2   Have each person, in turn tell the group about their ideal room.
3   Other topics which can be used include:

   * ideal holiday,
   * ideal garden,
   * ideal house,
   * ideal way to travel.

Comment

Do make clear to the group that the emphasis is not on producing a perfect drawing but on expressing their ideas and thoughts through drawing and painting. The exercise can be very useful and revealing, especially in residential care, to make staff aware of how each person likes their room and to make the accommodation more suitable for particular individuals.

P

Theme Collage

Materials

Magazines, scissors, glue and a large sheet of paper.

Preparation

Collect together a large variety of magazines.

Procedure

Have the group choose a theme, such as a season of the year, holidays, happiness, a beautiful house, sport, famous people or plants. When a theme has been chosen, have group members look through the magazines and cut out any pictures which represent their perception of the theme. Once the pictures have been cut out, get the group to organise and glue them on the large sheet of paper to form a collage. When the collage is complete, hold it up so everyone can see it. Give participants an opportunity to comment on the effect, how difficult it was to find the pictures, why they chose their particular pictures and what their feelings are about the overall effect. The picture can later be displayed on a wall for everyone to enjoy.

Variation

If the group is large, you could divide it into smaller groups of four or five people. You can then add more interest by having each group compose a collage using a different theme.

Comment

This is an activity which aids socialisation, stimulates creativity, involves decision making and encourages people to work together.

SECTION 5

Endings

Games which wind down, bring the session to an end
and reinforce what has been good.

I Enjoyed ...

Materials

Music and a machine to play it on.

Preparation

None.

Procedure

Ask each group member to think back over everything they have done during the session. It is helpful to state the activities in which everyone has taken part and recall a few of the incidents which have occurred while doing them. Now request that each person, in turn, state something they enjoyed during the period together. It may be the music, one of the activities, getting to know someone new, remembering something from the past, being in company or an appreciation of something said by someone else.

Variation

Introduce music into the proceedings. When the music stops, someone states something they enjoyed during the session. Repeat this until everyone in the group has had a chance to speak.

Comment

This exercise encourages the expression of appreciation. We are all, too often, good at being critical or looking at the negative, especially when feeling low in mood. This game reminds people that they have enjoyed something.

How I'm Feeling Now

Materials

Flipchart and a magic marker.

Preparation

None.

Procedure

Bring the group members together in a circle. Invite each person, in turn, to share with the group how they are feeling now. This may be tired, hungry, mellow, comfortable, relaxed, and so on. Participants simply state how they feel, without anyone commenting.

Variation

Use this activity both to open the session and to end it. When it is used as a beginning, write up on a flipchart how each person feels, explore this a little and, when everyone has made their statement, turn the chart away so that it cannot be seen. When doing the exercise again at the end of the session, bring the chart out once more and see if anyone feels different now.

Comment

This is a simple activity which allows expression of feeling. For some people, just being able to state and share how they feel, even if it is sad, will be useful. When used as a closure, it is usually best to let each statement stand on its own without too much explanation – otherwise there is a danger that it will not be a closure.

P

Gifts

Materials

Cards and pens.

Preparation

None.

Procedure

Have everyone sit in a circle. Ask group members to look at the person sitting next to them on their right (or left). Ask them, now they have got to know the person better during the session, what imaginary gift they would like to give that person. This may be something the person likes which has become known during the session, something that would be useful to them or that it is imagined they would like. Possibilities could range from something tangible, like a new dress or a bunch of flowers, to a nice meal, happiness or patience. When time has been given to think, ask for a volunteer to tell their neighbour what gift they wish for them. Continue in this manner until everyone has been wished a gift.

Variation

Give everyone in the group a card and a pen. Ask them to write the gift they wish to give to their neighbour on the card. When this task is completed, have everyone hand the cards to their neighbour at the same time. Complete the process by having each person state what gift they have been given.

Comment

This exercise always leaves the group members feeling good.

Private Thoughts

Materials

Pens and paper.

Preparation

None.

Procedure

Ask the group members to sit quietly for a moment and think of someone who is important to them. This could be a partner, a neighbour, a son or a friend. Now request that each person cast their mind back over what the group has been doing and how it has felt being in the group. Next, ask them to decide on something that they would like to share with that important person. Make it clear that they will not be asked to share their private thoughts. However, do invite them to tell the group the person they would like to share their thoughts with. Encourage members to give the reason why they chose that person.

Variation

Give each person a pen and some paper and invite them to write a letter to a person who is important in their life and share something about the group with them. Make it clear that the contents of the letter will remain private.

Comment

Knowing that they will not be asked to share their private thoughts with the group will enable participants to be honest with themselves. There is no fear of offending or having their privacy invaded. It will also enable them to gain some insight about themselves.

P

Feedback

Materials

None.

Preparation

None.

Procedure

Have an open discussion about how the group went. What did participants enjoy? What was it that made it enjoyable? What did they dislike? Why? What would they have liked done differently to make the activity more enjoyable in the future? How did doing the activities make them feel? Were the instructions clear? Did the group go on too long or not long enough? What would they like changed? Give plenty of opportunity for all to express themselves.

Variation

Invite each person, one at a time, to give feedback on how the session went for them.

Comment

Note the difference in the way each person experienced the group and use the information for future sessions. It is best not to allow people to dispute or disagree when getting feedback. Each person states their feeling or experience of the group and different views are respected.

Statements

Materials

Pens, paper, a bag a flipchart and magic marker.

Preparation

Write on separate pieces of paper the beginning of a statement relating to the time spent together. You will need one for each group member. Examples:

> **What interested me most was ...**

> **What I disliked most was ...**

> **The funniest thing was ...**

> **What made me smile was ...**

> **The person I would like to get to know better is ...**

> **I was irritated when ...**

> **I was nervous when ...**

> **What I would like to do more of is ...**

> **The kindest person to me was ...**

Procedure

Put all the slips of paper into a bag. Invite each group member to draw one out and to complete the statement in writing. Explain that the statement must relate to the time spent together. When everyone has done this, collect all the pieces of paper and put them back in the bag again. Now have each person take a piece of paper from the bag. Ask a volunteer to read out what is written on their paper. Continue in this fashion until all the statements have been read out.

Variation

Prepare the beginnings of about five statements. Write the first one up on a flipchart. Now have a round with each person in the group completing the statement aloud. Write the beginning of a second statement up on the flipchart. Follow the same procedure until all five statements have been completed by everyone.

Comment

You can compose the statements to draw out any information you want from the group. The activity can be made easier by reducing the number of statements to be completed.

What I Wanted ... What I Got

Materials

A flipchart and magic marker, pens and paper.

Preparation

None.

Procedure

Write up the following beginnings of statements on the flip chart:

* What I wanted from the group today was ...
* What I got from the group today was ...
* What I want from future groups is ...

Give each person, in turn, an opportunity to complete each statement verbally. When this has been done, encourage some general discussion about what has been said.

Variation

Split the group up into two or three smaller groups. Give them time to discuss the statements and write down a combined response on paper. Circulate as necessary to give support. When the task has been completed, bring everyone back together again and have an elected person from each group give feedback to the whole group.

Comment

A very useful exercise, this enables the group leader to get feedback. It also enables group members to feel that they can influence and have some control over what happens.

What I Like About ...

Materials

None.

Preparation

None.

Procedure

Bring everyone into a circle. Ask each participant to consider the person on their right and think of something that they like about them. After allowing a moment for thought, start the process by making a statement about the person on your right, beginning with the words, 'What I like about'. An example might be 'What I like about Barry is his thoughtfulness.' That person now turns to the person on his right and makes a statement about that person in the same manner. This continues round the group.

Variations

1 Instead of focusing on individuals, have everyone make a similar statement about the group. The statement would begin with the words; 'What I like about the group is'.
2 Have a round of both types of statement.

Comment

This is a good way of ending the group on a very positive and uplifting note. Some participants may feel slight embarrassment at praising others or being praised, and may need a little encouragement. However, it always ensures that the group ends with a good feeling.

Simple Relaxation

Materials

Soft, relaxing music.

Preparation

None.

Procedure

Ensure that everyone is sitting comfortably and that their clothes are loose. Switch on the music and tell them to close their eyes. Ask them to think of something relaxing. This may be the sound of the sea, a word like 'calm', a picture they like, a place such as a waterfall or stream, a quiet country scene or a flower. Explain that, as they concentrate, they will feel their muscles and bodies relax. Tension will drain away from their foreheads, eyes, mouth and jaw, through the neck, shoulders, down their chests and backs, through their arms and from their fingertips. Tensions will sink through their hips, thighs, calves, feet and toes into the floor.

Remind everyone to concentrate on their scene and repeat the instructions slowly. Do this two or three times. When you finish, ask everyone to sit quietly for a moment and listen to the music. Next, ask them to open their eyes, still sitting quietly, and gradually reorient themselves to the room. Do not allow anyone to stand up or move around immediately.

Variation

Simply play the music for a few minutes, asking everyone to close their eyes, relax and enjoy the music.

Comment

Simplicity is often the best. A simple relaxation exercise is always an excellent way to end and leave everyone feeling good.

What I'm Taking Away

Materials

Flipchart and a magic marker.

Preparation

None.

Procedure

Write up the words, 'What I'm taking away' on the flipchart. Ask all the group members to reflect on the time spent together. It may be helpful for some groups if you mention a few of the things which have happened during the session – sharing of anecdotes, good-humoured banter, memories and experience, and so on. After a moment for reflection, ask each person, in turn, to state what they are taking away from the group. This could be a sense of companionship, courage, a pleasant time spent together, a feeling of being cheered up, amusing memories and so on.

Variation

Instead of going round the group, with members making statements one by one, have them shout out at random what they are taking away. Write the statements up on the flipchart as they are called out.

Comment

This is another pleasant way to end a group and help participants to acknowledge the benefits gained.

What I Have Learned

Materials

Flipchart and magic marker.

Preparation

None.

Procedure

Write up on the flipchart the words, 'What I have learned'. Next, request that each person reflect on the group proceedings. If necessary, jog memories by stating one or two of the things which individuals may have learned during the group. After a moment for reflection, have everyone state something they have learned during the session. This may be someone's name that they did not know, a piece of news, information about something, a new way to do something, how to play a game or do a helpful exercise, and so on. Write each statement up on the flipchart and be amazed.

Variation

Do a round of 'What I have achieved'. This could include, 'lifted my left arm to shoulder height, made a new friend, talked to someone I did not know before, expressed my opinion, said how I felt', and so on.

Comment

This is another closure which helps participants acknowledge benefits gained from the group.

What I Feel Good About is ...

Materials

Flipchart and magic marker.

Preparation

None.

Procedure

Write up the words, 'What I feel good about is' on the flipchart. Give everyone a moment to reflect and then ask each person, in turn, to make a personal statement beginning with the words written on the flipchart. The statement may or may not be confined to what has been happening in the session. The statements can be written up on the flipchart.

Variation

A round of 'What I feel bad about is ...' can be combined with a round of 'What I feel good about is ....' However, when doing this, make sure that you do the round of 'What I feel bad about is ...' first. Otherwise, there may be danger of leaving the group on a negative note.

Comment

If anyone has difficulty thinking of something positive to say, you can always remind them of something good which happened in the group.

What I Value About Myself is ...

Materials

Flipchart and magic marker, pens and paper, a bag.

Preparation

None.

Procedure

Have everyone sit in a circle. Write the words 'What I value about myself is ...' on the flipchart, so that it can be seen by all. Now ask each person to think about something they value about themselves. After allowing a moment for thought, ask for a volunteer to make a statement beginning with those words. This might be 'What I value about myself is that I am a good friend', ' ... I've got a good sense of humour', '... I'm good at art', '... I don't give up easily', '.... I'm a hard worker', and so on. Encourage participants, where appropriate, to expand a little on their statements.

Variation

1   To make this into a longer activity have each person write down their statement on a piece of paper. Put the completed statements in a bag. Invite participants to take a piece of paper out at random. Each person now reads out a statement and the other members of the group guess who has written it.

2   Some people find it very difficult to make positive statements about themselves. It can be helpful sometimes to have a short brainstorming session at the beginning of the exercise with participants shouting out the sort of things that people might value about themselves. Write these up on the flipchart and then have individuals choose one which they feel applies to them.

Comment

This is a good activity for reinforcing a positive self-image.

Social Drinks

Materials

Drinks and biscuits.

Preparation

Prepare a selection of drinks and biscuits, ready to hand out.

Procedure

Invite group members to help with handing round the drinks and biscuits. Encourage everyone to chat and comment about the group. Is anyone missing from the session? Are they away on holiday? Is anyone doing anything special before the group meets again? Do group members want to send a card if a person is unwell? Talk about what has been planned for the next session. Go round and speak to each group member, shake hands, ask them how they felt about today's group, reassure them that it was good to have the time together. Invite other group members to do the same.

Variation

Use the discussion to decide what everyone would like to do in the next session.

Comment

This is a very natural way to end a session. Inviting group members to help give out the drinks and biscuits provides a role for individuals and a chance to think of others.

Musical Endings

Materials

A pleasant music tape, record or CD and a machine to play it on.

Preparation

None.

Procedure

Make sure that each person is sitting comfortably. Start playing the music and ask participants to close their eyes and relax. Now suggest that they think about what they have enjoyed during the session. Let the music continue for a few moments and then have everyone open their eyes. Give a few seconds for participants to orient themselves to the room again and ask each person, in turn, to state how they feel.

Variation

Ask different group members to bring in favourite pieces of music each week. Simply play these as a way of relaxing at the end of the group.

Comment

Having group members bring their own music helps them 'own' and identify with activities and encourages initiative.

Massage

Materials

A music tape, record or CD and a machine to play it on.

Preparation

None.

Procedure

Have the group members split into pairs with one person standing behind the other. Switch on the music. Next, starting at the base of the neck, the person behind begins massaging the person in front: first the neck, then the shoulders, moving to the centre of the back. They should massage outwards with each hand, or in circles, finally brushing downwards to the waist. They do this a few times and then partners switch roles.

Variation

1 Have the group members form a circle facing inwards. Ask everyone to turn to the right. Now instruct each person to massage the back of the person in front of them.
2 Instead of a straightforward massage, tell them to build a runway on the back in front of them: first the group members clear the ground of scrub by using a plucking motion, then they pat the ground flat. Once this has been done for a moment or two, they smooth the surface using the palms of their hands.

Comment

A simple but effective exercise, this leaves people with a nice, relaxed feeling. It can also help to improve circulation or digestion and to reduce pain in rheumatic conditions.

> **Do bear in mind, when using the exercise, that some people may be unused to physical contact and find it difficult initially to touch or be touched.**

Establish comfort by first using other activities which involve less touching.

Before I Leave

Materials

None.

Preparation

None.

Procedure

Form the group into a circle and invite participants, one by one, to complete the statement 'Before I leave ...'. They might say:

* 'I would like to thank everybody for being such good company.'
* 'I would like to thank you for cheering me up.'
* 'I would like to thank John for bringing in the music.'
* 'I would like to thank Ivy for bringing in the photographs.'

Variation

Have group members complete a sentence beginning, 'I appreciate ...'.

Comment

A simple exercise, this leaves a really positive feeling. If necessary, remind participants about enjoyable events during the group or how they have helped each other.

Helps and Hinders

Materials

Flipchart and magic marker.

Preparation

None.

Procedure

Write the beginning of two sentences on the flip chart: 'It hinders me when ...' and 'It helps me when ...'. Ask the group members to think about the two statements and how they can complete them. Then ask each person, in turn, to complete the statements. They might say, 'It hinders me when everyone talks at once. I can't hear anyone properly. It helps me when one person speaks at a time and I can see who is speaking.' Encourage individuals to enlarge on their statements as appropriate, so that they can be understood by everyone.

Variation

Use the beginnings, 'What I would like to change is ...' and 'What I would like to leave the same is ...'.

Comment

Often individuals' progress or enjoyment in the group can be hindered by things which are simple to change, but they never get the opportunity to state them. Once they are known, the group leader and other group members can ensure that any difficulties anyone has are taken into account.

Saying Farewell

Materials

None.

Preparation

None.

Procedure

Divide the group into an inner and outer circle with an equal number of people in each. Those in the inner circle face those in the outer circle. Ask each couple to shake hands and say some sort of farewell such as:

* 'I have enjoyed our time together',
* 'It has been nice meeting you',
* 'I really enjoyed the poem you read', or
* 'It was lovely talking to you'.

On the word 'change', the inner circle moves round one place to the right to face the next person on the outer circle and each person says farewell in a similar manner again. This continues until everyone has said 'farewell' to everyone else.

Variation

Instead of forming an inner and outer circle, split the group into pairs. This time, on the word 'change', everyone finds a new partner to say farewell.

Comment

It is always pleasant to be told someone has enjoyed your company. It produces a good feeling.

P

Session Review

Materials

A roll of wallpaper, or several flipchart sheets joined together, and a magic marker.

Preparation

None.

Procedure

Attach a length of wallpaper (or the flipchart sheets) to a wall. Draw a thick line along the centre of the length of wallpaper. This line represents the time spent together in the session. Mark the different games or activities participated in by the group along the line, with a cross for each event, and write beside each cross what it represents. Now ask participants to shout out their comments about each event and write them on the chart – positive comments above the line, negative comments below the line. If appropriate, encourage players to write their comments themselves. Comments made by one person will trigger reactions from others which can then be added.

When everyone has commented on each event, give an opportunity to discuss the total session. Studying the chart will show that it has been enjoyed by all, most or only some participants. Does it indicate any changes that need to be made for the next session? Discuss and agree on any suggestions for change.

Variation

Make the chart a collage by adding practical examples of work completed by the group: for example, writing a verse from a poem which has been read out, attaching drawings or a cartoon depicting an exercise and so on.

Comment

This is a good method for collecting reactions, opinions and suggestions from the whole group. It can also provide a good learning process for the group leader.

Alphabetical List of Games